Electrician Tool Pouch

Double Your Sales by Getting
Your Online and Print Marketing Right

FIRST
EDITION

Albert Glenn Ozburn

Electrician's Marketing Tool Pouch
Double Your Sales by Getting Your Online and Print Marketing Right

by Albert Glenn Ozburn
Copyright © 2020 by Albert Glenn Ozburn.
All rights reserved.

Publisher: Get Viral! Marketing, LLC., 85 River Birch Drive, Oxford, GA 30054

www.PowerSurgeSEO.com is a division of Get Viral! Marketing, LLC. located at www.GetViralMarketing.com.

ISBN: 978-0-578-77716-0

Table of Contents

Introduction

In this book, I are going to show you how to effectively market your electrical business (or any other business) either online or through print marketing. I am really excited about what I have to share here. The information that you are about to study is good, solid, reliable information that, if implemented correctly, can have an impact on the growth of your electrical services company. This information is not a secret but you would have to pry this amount of information from most marketers and it would literally take months to obtain all of this information from sources online. *It is just that valuable!*

I do want to warn you that marketing can be tough and has become tougher over the years. It's similar to fishing. You can prepare for a great day of fishing and sometimes the fish just don't bite. The various strategies used in marketing are similar to the bait that you use when you fish. You can cast your line from 20 different fishing poles using 20 different types of baits or lures. If you are lucky, you will catch a fish on all 20 poles with the 20 different lures. In marketing, you cast the lines out and see which lure (strategy) is working best. Just because a strategy works good this month doesn't mean it will work good next month. A good marketing strategy is similar to fishing whereas it requires skill, repetitiveness, endurance, trial and error, time, and patience. If those traits are not in your wheelhouse, you may want to think about finding a marketing agency to talk to. If you think you can deliver these traits, marketing your electrical services business may be attainable for you. Whatever you decide, try to remain a part of the marketing decisions. If you decide an agency is a better fit, interview and hire the agency **that best fits what's in this book.** Afterwards, please stay in touch with them bi-weekly to make sure they are doing their job. If you like the "DIY" approach, be diligent and steadfast and never give up hope because good things come to those who wait and work hard. **If, at anytime, you become disappointed, always remember that you can send an email to us at help@powersurgeseo.com or call us at 1-888-235-4SEO (4736). We will be glad to help in any way.**

First Things First

Before we start on your electrical marketing makeover, we need to get a few things hashed out.

First and foremost, we need to tweak a few things, most notably, between your ears. When it comes to marketing, it has to be a well-planned out and a methodical way of promoting you and your electrical business. This is not something that will miraculously take place overnight. Online organic marketing, and even print marketing, can take months, if not years, to evolve into the perfect marketing strategy. In marketing, there is the option of "quicker" marketing that is extremely expensive. This type of marketing, often referred to as "pay-per-click" (PPC) and "pay-per-lead" (PPL), will be discussed later. The plan that we propose is a marketing plan combined with a strong organic SEO base accentuated by some PPC and maybe some PPL. This strategy is based on years of experience in marketing companies just like yours.

When it comes to marketing, there are many, many questions that can be asked and perhaps there is no "one" answer. Each specific question requires a well-thought out answer to validate your present marketing strategy and how it can be improved upon.

Later on in this book, I will give you a series of questions that will help you determine where you are in marketing your electrical company, but for now, the most important thing to note is that you have to have a clear head and open mind when inquiring about marketing. You need to know that, unlike the electrical profession, sometimes marketing, especially organic marketing, may take longer to evolve or to actually show a "Return On Investment" (ROI). One thing is for sure though. If you follow the recommendations noted in this book, you will most likely succeed in your marketing strategy.

"One thing common with every single electrical job is the fact that when the job is finished, the job is finished and you get to go to the next job."

For example, a new commercial electrical job, depending on the size and extent, may take your company anywhere from 2-6 months or more, after starting, to complete the electrical wiring portion of the project. One thing common with every single electrical job is the fact that when the job is finished, the job is finished and you get to go to the next job. When you are wiring a new location, you have the electrical blueprints to help "walk" you though the plans and help you formulate an internal game plan of how you and your team will start and work the job. Usually before you even win the bid, you have to meet with the <u>General Contractor</u> (GC) and have a mandatory walk through just to be able to bid on the job. Then there are the countless hours of estimating the job. Once you submit and win the bid, you then have to meet job milestones, start rough-ins, attend inspector walk-throughs, and much more while making the GC (your customer) happy. Now translate that into marketing. You are now the GC and the "electrical contractor" is your marketing agency.

Whereas electrical has a starting point and a finite ending point, marketing has so many "ebbs and flows" with an ever evolving internet that you have to continually stay abreast of. Daily algorithmic changes, rules and regulations, and much more seem to dictate the marketer's strategies and life. This is not to say that you, as an owner/electrician, can't market your own company but rather to say that your time is valuable and may be better spent doing the things that you know best - electrical services.

This book is written with the intent to lead and guide you, as an owner/electrician, to incorporate the most fundamental ways to market your own electrical company into your marketing plan. This book, although well planned and conceived, is not the perfect book nor does it have all of the answers for your specific marketing needs. This book, however, does provide the fundamentals of marketing that will help you understand how to better market your company and realize the various marketing strategies that the internet offers. **After reading this book you will either have enough knowledge to carry out your own marketing plan or you will have the knowledge to talk sensibly to a marketing**

professional and understand the marketing plan that they may lay before you. Suffice it to say, after reading this book, you may even know more than the majority of "marketing professionals" that you seek advice from. My wish for you and your company is for you to grow immensely (or at least grow to your desires) after reading and studying this book.

About The Author

Before I get to deep, I would like to introduce myself to you. My name is Glenn "Ozzie" Ozburn and I am the owner of ***www.PowerSurgeSEO. com,*** a marketing company devoted to electricians like you.

I grew up probably like most of you. I had to work hard for everything that I have and never got anything handed to me. Matter of fact, I grew up on a farm and both my mom and dad instilled (with the help of a stiff, swift discipine) a work ethic in me and my siblings that is, basically, second to none.

We were mainly small vegetable farmers (corn and peas) but we also farmed cotton in my younger days. When I say small, we still farmed many acres of vegetables by my high school days. I didn't know it then, but looking back, those were actually some of the best days of my life and I still often find myself yearning to be back on a farm. Living and working on a farm taught me many of the values that I have instilled in my life even today.

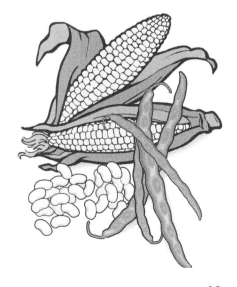

Although my family spent a lot of time working the farm, my older brother, Terry, eventually had the opportunity to study to become an electrician. After receiving his journeyman's electrical license, he eventually opened up his own electrical business. That was also the start of my journey as an electrician's helper as I worked myself though college, attending the University of Georgia where I studied Photographic Design. After college, my career led me into the graphics, prepress and the printing trade and over the years I became the Lead Electronics Assembly Operator for a company that represented many Fortune 100 manufacturers, including Coca-

Mom & Dad circa late 50's, early 60's

Cola North America, Unilever, Procter & Gamble and many more. I actually became an expert in all things "packaging and labeling". This expertise morphed over into the digital marketing sphere so I then started my own small boutique marketing agency, Get Viral! Marketing, LLC., which eventually spun into an "electricians only" niche marketing agency named **Power Surge SEO (www.PowerSurgeSEO.com)**.

In a sense, I have come full circle back to my roots of electrical work. I'm not necessarily wiring up panels or threading rigid pipe, but I am solely concentrating on helping electrical business grow by educating electricians and their businesses with the latest marketing techniques. Now that you know me, I hope you can, as an electrician or business owner, put your trust into what you are about to read in my book. I will try not to bore you and will perhaps add a little humor but more than anything I want to educate you about advertising and marketing and make it where you can enjoy learning about growing your business via the internet. If you like what you read, please share your "like" with others by leaving me (my company - Power Surge SEO) and this book a good Google or Amazon review. All in all, this book is not about me but it is about empowering you to take the next step in growing your business. I want both of us to succeed in business and more importantly in life.

About Our Company. Power Surge SEO

...and what we do at Power Surge SEO:

Our company, www.PowerSurgeSEO.com, excels in everything noted in this book. If you need it done, we can do it and more. We specialize in helping electrical contractors and electricians manage their internet marketing, their print media marketing, and much more. We will design, develop and setup your website, making sure that it is optimized for SEO (search engine optimization), write content for you, blog for you, manage your social media for you, develop your website's authority over the internet via citations and directories, link build, review management, reputation management, track your online rankings, and more.

We will basically put the strategies outlined in this book into action for you and your business with minimal interaction on your part.

Our team is based in the good old USA. We are a real brick and mortar operation with a team of exceptional young and older men and women who have been doing this type of work for many years.

Our team consist of customer success maners (CSM), writers, web designers, videographers, photographers, link builders, graphic designers and many more experts in their related field. We will be more than happy to work with you and help you build the electrical services company that you dream of.

Call us today at
1-888-235-4SEO (4736)
www.PowerSurgeSEO.com

We would love the opportunity to work with you **but that is not the reason that I wrote this book.** I wrote this book because I know that there are thousands of electrical business owners out there that either just don't know where to start or feel like they're at a disadvantage when they talk to a marketing agency. I want to educate you and give you enough knowledge to have a little leverage in life. I want you to take the following information and implement it, hopefully achieving much success along the way. This book has always been a passion of mine. Not necessarily to help electricians to achieve great marketing results, but to be able to help others along the way. My passion is to help people and I would like that to be my legacy for my children and my name.

When reading this book, you will occasionally see a "Notes" section as below. Feel free to take notes and refer back as often as needed.

Notes

_____
_____
_____
_____
_____
_____
_____
_____

What's a Marketing Plan?

Many electrical contractors and business owners, in general, think that marketing involves setting up a website and waiting for the traffic to roll in, but things aren't that simple. There is this "necessary evil" called marketing that you have to attend to. In order for your company's marketing to really work, you need to have a comprehensive marketing plan in place. That doesn't mean you need to spend thousands of dollars on an ad agency but rather you need to have a structured business marketing plan going forward. With this book, you can do everything yourself or, at the least, have guidance to know what needs to be done and then hire the most qualified professionals to do the job for you at a fair price.

I'm going to let you in on some of the secrets that you can do to make the most of your company's marketing strategy. You're going to learn how to use your website properly, how to use your online presence to stay in touch with current customers and develop loyalty, while also bring in new customers. You will learn how to get more traffic to your business either online or through sophisticated "print" marketing. Yes, you heard me right! I did say print marketing. Today, print may be on life support, but if done properly, you can still achieve great results with a local, targeted print-on-paper campaign.

So let's get started, shall we?

"Give me six hours to chop down a tree and I will spend the first four sharpening the axe."
- Abraham Lincoln

Abraham Lincoln's quote applies to more than just chopping down a tree. It applies to a well-thought out marketing strategy. A marketing strategy is similar to a *house foundation*. Like a foundation, you are going to build upon it. You need to carefully think it out and seek advice if you have to. Basically, you will now be building your business upon a sound marketing foundation. Not to say that you can't change it, unlike a physical, solid concrete foundation, a marketing strategy can be fluid and actually needs to be fluid and changeable to survive. Houses get remodeled all the time, but they are still sitting upon that sound basic foundation. The knowledge that you gain by reading this book will be your sound marketing foundation. Read on and I will give you recommendations on how to build your marketing strategy or "foundation".

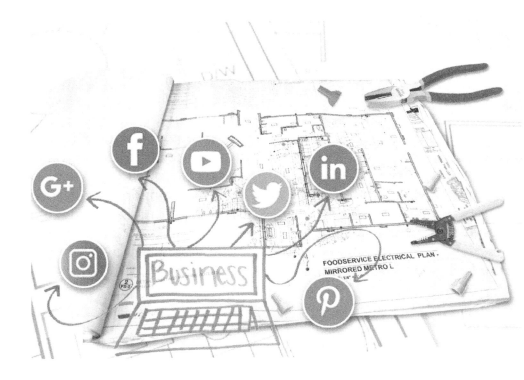

What is a "marketing plan or strategy"? … *I'm glad you asked.*

The technological definition for a "marketing plan or strategy" can be a simple or comprehensive plan for the sole purpose of achieving set marketing objectives of your company or business. In layman's terms, it's a plan and more specifically, a written out plan. A plan similar to what you get from your general contractor just before you start the job of wiring the building. As an electrical contractor, it would be fruitless for you to start working on a new residential, commercial or industrial build without the proper blueprints. We all know that an electrician will need the properly designed electrical schematics to wire a retail location properly. It only makes sense that you apply the same requirements to working on a job as to creating your very own marketing plan. A well thought out marketing plan provides a blueprint for attaining your company's marketing objectives. It is the building block of a marketing plan.

A "marketing strategy" can be as simple as a few details drawn out on a napkin at the local coffee house, or it can be as detailed as the well executed and engineered blueprints for a large retail location. Neither one is wrong or right but your strategy depends on several factors. *Is this a long-term marketing strategy or short-term marketing strategy? Do you only want a few more customers or do you want to be flooded with customers? Do you want to spend a lot of time or only a short amount of time with marketing?* This list of questions can go on and on but suffice it to say, a well thought-out, organized and detailed marketing strategy will win out everyday.

A great marketing strategy helps a company, such as yours, to concentrate it's scarce (or many) resources on the best possible opportunities so as to increase the sales. Just a reminder, resources can mean more than just money. I have seen many people who have spent thousands of dollars a month going down the wrong marketing "rabbit hole". In contrast, I have also seen many frugal individuals spend a lot less and have gotten a much better return on their investment (ROI) from marketing wisely. I hope to help you market wisely as to receive a better "ROI".

I once witnessed the owner of an Urgent Care facility spend $8,000 a month for PPC. When that didn't work, the big, well-known marketing agency (named after a dangerous arachnid) advised the owner that to get more customers, they needed to increase the PPC ad spend, to well over $10,000 a month.

That didn't work neither!

Times have changed and long gone are the days of expensive print only marketing only to be substituted with expensive online marketing. Small and medium-sized businesses need to be keenly aware of the importance of promotional and marketing strategies, be it online or print, that help your organization utilize the skills of your employees and can help you easily develop creative approaches to sales and customer service.

As an electrical contractor, it would be fruitless for you to start working on a new residential, commercial or industrial build without the proper blueprints. An electrician will need the electrical schematics to wire a location properly just like a plumber will need blueprints to know where to install the plumbing. It only makes sense that you apply the same requirements in creating your very own marketing plan. A well thought out marketing plan provides a blueprint for attaining your company's marketing objectives. It is the building block of a marketing plan.

A "marketing strategy" should be built upon a sound foundation. In general, your marketing foundation will be built upon your brand, website, online and offline presence, and more. A sound, or unsound, marketing foundation will shape your day-to-day marketing activities, effective spending habits, and could lead to an effective marketing campaign with a great return on investment or be a total "waste of money".

After you have read this book, we hope that you will be able to carefully chart out your marketing strategy and be able to successfully answer these and many more questions without hesitation.

Do you have a clear, up-to-date brand that properly identifies your company and services?

Do you have a clear brand that consistently generates the same "brand" image for consumers to immediately know who you are and the services that you provide?

Does your brand have a consistent look and feel across all media, print, digital, signage?

How does your website compare to the competition? Tip: Google "electrician [your primary region/city]" e.g., "Electrician Dothan Alabama," and compare.

Looking at your strategy or existing website, are there any barriers in your prospects' path toward becoming customers? For example, as a electrician, do you offer automation and controls installation? As an electrician, could you also offer HVAC? As an electrical contractor, can you also offer Mechanical work?

Do you know how to measure the success of your marketing investment?

Do you have a solid and solidified strategy for business development and marketing related to it?

> **Don't worry, I am only asking these questions to get you thinking. You don't have to answer them yet!**

> *"There is only one winning strategy. It is to carefully define the target market and direct a superior offering to that target market."* - Philip Kotler

The following two pages contain just a few important questions that I really need for you to think over and answer to the best of your ability. Your answers will help us later in devising your marketing plan. *We will go into more details later but relax, concentrate and fill out this information.*

Your Business Information

Legal Company Name (Legal name on paper):

_____

Common Company Name (what's on the letter head and business cards):

_____

Company Slang Names: (the shortened version or what people know the name of your company as)

_____

_____

_____

_____

Company Headquarters: (Physical Address - no PO Boxes)

_____

_____

_____

_____

Other Company Locations: (you can list towns are cities, no addresses for now)

_____

_____

_____

_____

Your Company Phone Number(s):

_____

Is your Company Phone Number(s) used by another company or different type of service other than electrical?   Circle: Yes   No
If 'Yes", explain:

_____
_____
_____
_____

Website
Do you have a website? ❏ Yes   ❏ No

If you have a website, talk about how you would like your website to look or how you would improve it.

_____
_____
_____
_____
_____
_____
_____

As the owner of an electrical services company, list out every possible service that you will offer to your customer. (for example, Industrial automation and controls, residential landscape lighting, warehouse LED lighting upgrades, etc.,)

_____
_____
_____
_____

As you read this book, you will then understand the importance of why I am asking you these questions!

Google - the New Phone Book

Back many years ago, a potential client only had one real source to find a service company like yours and that was through the "Yellow Pages". There were a few other sources such as newspaper  ads, printed media that someone had placed under your car's windshield wiper while you shopped (ha ha), the old resealable sandwich bag (enclosed with a rock and your business card) placed on top of your mailbox, etc. Some of those old marketing plans may still be viable to a certain degree but "the times have changed" and your marketing plan needs to change for you to be able to survive.

Here is an amazing statistic that may suggest to you that it is indeed "time to change". Did you know that in 2020, according to Google Ads, 97% of consumers go online to find and research local products and services?

"97% of consumers go online to find and research local products and services."

Here are some more amazing facts that you may have not known.

Over 75% of consumers think that marketing has changed more in the last 6 years than all of the prior 50 years combined! <u>That is a staggering fact.</u>

Do you realize that today's modern consumers spends 8.8 hours a day, on average, engaging with digital content, and most of that is on their smart phone or mobile device.

Most of these consumers have at least one thing in common. They love doing their initial search for home or business improvements through Google searches and they love searching on their phones.

Did you know that...

- High-quality content (blogging, content, press releases, etc.,) and link building (citations, directories, linkwheels, backlinks, etc.,) are the two most important signals used by Google to rank your website for search.

- *According to Google Ads*, **there are more than 500,000 online searches for "electricians" each month.**

- *According to Google Ads*, there are more than 1.2 million online searches for roofing services each month.

- *According to Google Ads*, there are more than 4.2 million online searches for home builders and design-build firms each month.

- *According to Google Ads*, there are more than 2.8 million online searches for plumbers each month.

- *According to Google Ads*, there are more than 660,000 online searches for remodelers each month.

- *According to Google Ads*, there are more than 1.7 million online searches for contractors each month.

- 70-80% of consumers research a company online before visiting a business or contractor or before making a purchase from them.

- 82% of consumers use their smartphones when searching for a local business.

- Most consumers do not trust reviews more than 3 months old.

- 45% of Americans believe that Jeffrey Epstein didn't kill himself.

- 100% of American's car warranties have expired - per daily robocall. To file a complaint with the FCC, go to consumercomplaints.fcc.gov.

- 82% of people who implemented an SEO strategy found it to be effective.

What I have listed here is only a snapshot of what is out there on the internet. I am showing you these facts to help "condition" your mind that digital, online marketing is here to stay and you need to embrace it if you want your business to survive. The facts are amazing when you really study them and I want to show you how to use these facts (and the internet) to your advantage. Back in the old days (prior to 2008 and the inception of the "smart phone"), although the telephone book was on life support, it was still the most viable way to find a contractor or service provider for your project. Nowadays, "the finger does the clickin" instead of "the walking".

Marketing Explained

Now that we have "somewhat" introduced you to the concept and the idea of a marketing plan, let's briefly analyze marketing.

For the next few days, building your marketing plan will be a *"work in progress"*. I say that because, unless you are already a marketing expert, you will need to learn the basic marketing "vernacular" as well as a few marketing concepts. The first part of this section will be discussing more about marketing terms and what they mean. In the next section, you will see my "Pyramid of Marketing" in all of it's Egyptian glory. Some may look at this and say that it is overkill. Others will say that it is not enough. The way that I look at it is these methods are proven over and over. If you want to take the "Pyramid of Marketing" and add to it, go for it! If you want to take away from it, go for it! I am just trying to give you several options, in order of importance, to incorporate into your marketing plan. I suggest that you at least immediately try to incorporate the bottom three layers of SEO, social media, and online directories. Once you get these going in the right direction, you can then incorporate other layers but not necessarily in any order.

> *"Marketing is a Race without a Finishing Line."*
> — Philip Kotler

Marketing Terminology

Before we get entrenched into your custom marketing plans, here are just a few of the words that you will hear when speaking or reading about marketing your electrical business. I will not list every single marketing term because most will not apply to you. Most will apply to the people that you hire to get the work done. As long as you know the basics, you will have enough knowledge to keep marketers from taking advantage of you.

Some of these terms you may find that you will use daily while others you may never hear about or utter again. Please read over the following terminology carefully to help you understand the rest of the book. All in all, this will give you a much better understanding of marketing and also help you understand marketing "speak". Please understand that by reading this book, it is just the beginning of your marketing experience. Today's marketing is dynamic, fluid and ever changing. As much as you learn about marketing, there is much, much more to learn and you will never learn it all. I only mention this to show you the importance of you taking your marketing serious. If you are unwilling to take it serious, hire a vetted professional that will.

Marketing terms in alphabetical order:

A/B Testing

Testing two versions of a webpage, email subject line, landing page, CTA, etc. to see which one performs better. "A" may represent the subject line of one email and "B" may be a totally different subject line with same email. These tests are performed to see how the recipient react. Some will react to the "A" email while others will react to the "B" email. It's all in how you word the Subject Line.

Above the Fold

"Above the Fold" is an old newspaper term (fold of newspaper) that refers to the part of the website that is viewable when you first open the site. This is the top portion of the website before you have to scroll. Ideally you want to have very important information "above the fold" so that viewers see it immediately.

Advertising

Putting a spotlight on a product, service or business through paid broadcasting – print media or digital media.

Analytics

Tracking and recording data and creating meaningful patterns from it to better understand your marketing endeavors. This helps to inform and educate you and determine future marketing behaviors or endeavors. The data can come from website traffic, conversions, social media, etc.

Google Analytics - above - is a common way to view data.

Artificial Intelligence (AI)

A computer, machine, or software system or process that can mimic certain aspects of human intellect. You will see it being used more and more to predict human behavior. This is also used for predicting buying and spending habits. AI programs may be able to display image perception, reasoning and voice recognition.

Backlinks

Backlinks are links from one website to a page on another website. Google and other major search engines consider backlinks "votes" for a specific page. Websites and Website Pages with a high number of backlinks tend to have high (SERP) organic search engine rankings. Backlinks are also known as "inbound links", "incoming links" or "one way links".

Tier-One (Tier-1) Backlinks are links you earn or build directly to your website.

<u>Tier-Two (Tier-2)</u> are links that directly pass the ranking value to tier-one links. Google sees tier-two links as a "good" support of tier-one links.

With this "pyramid" backlinks structure, each layer of links reinforces the top layer, making Tier 1 the strongest of the two tiers. Tier 2's backing of

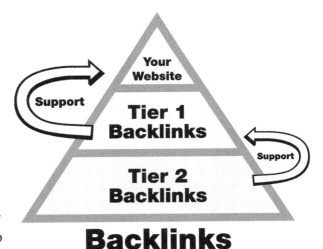

Tier 1 allows for a high concentration of authority to your website. Search engines see this as a "recommendation".

Baseline

The starting point from which comparisons are made for analysis, performance improvement, forecasting and strategy creation. For example, the average (baseline) normal body temperature is generally accepted as 98.6°F. It can fluctuate during times of sickness and even health but everyone has a "baseline" temperature.

Bingbot

Bingbot is a web-crawling robot, deployed by Microsoft. It is similar to Googlebot deployed by Google.

Blogging

Originally, the term was web log or weblog and eventually...blog. Individuals, some small business and even large corporations write articles, commentaries, and similar, publishing regularly on their website. Blogging is a primary component of the inbound marketing method, blogging helps to drive website traffic, builds thought leadership and authority, and drives leads. Blogging also tells authorities that you and your site is "still alive" and active.

Bounce Rate

The number of people who land on a page of your website and leave without clicking on anything before moving on to another page on your site. In email terminology, the bounce rate can be considered somewhat bad. You never want to have a "high" bounce rate when sending out emails to lists.

Brand

Anything that brings about awareness of a specific product, service or business while separating it from other establishments. Branding can be colors, quotes, and more. (Re)branding is reestablishing a previously branded product, service or business with a new "look" or "feel".

Business-to-Business (B2B)

Describing a business that markets or sells to other businesses. This really doesn't apply to you wiring a retail location but would apply if you made widgets and only sold your widgets to a retail business for resell.

Business-to-Consumer (B2C)

Describing a business that markets and sells to consumers. Walmart and Apple are two giants that practice B2C.

CAPTCHA - See "ReCaptcha"

CAN-SPAM

CAN-SPAM stands for "Controlling the Assault of Non-Solicited Pornography and Marketing." Passed in 2003, this U.S. law establishes the rules for commercial email and commercial messages, it gives email recipients the right to have a business stop emailing them, and also outlines the penalties incurred for those who violate the law. For example, CAN-SPAM is the reason businesses are required to have an "unsubscribe" option at the bottom of every email. CASL is the Canadian version of this law.

Call To Action

In marketing, a "call to action" is usually located on your website, webinar, podcast or an email. It is a piece of content or advice intended to induce a viewer, reader, or listener to perform a specific act, typically taking the form of an instruction or directive. The main goal of a "call to action" is to induce someone to eventually convert to your products and services. A "call to action" can be a phone number, an email address listed on a website, or even a "Buy Now" button on an eCommerce site.

Churn or Churn Rate

The percentage of customers who cancel a product or service or leave within a specified time period. For example, if you have 100 steady, monthly customers and the next month you lose 5 customers, your churn rate is 5% for that month.

Click-Through-Rate (CTR)

This number shows the visitors that move or "click" hyperlinks through your website or marketing campaigns. The Click-Through-Rate is also a metric that measures the number of clicks advertisers receive on their ads per number of impressions.

Cold Calling

Approaching prospective clients by phone or face-to-face without having ever had any interaction with them before. Since the inception of the Covid-19 pandemic, face-to face cold calling has become virtually impossible.

Cold email

Similar to "Cold Calling" but using email to interact with a prospect with whom they've had no prior contact. If this is done on a massive scale, you have to be aware and careful with anti-spam laws. (See CAN-SPAM)

Content

Information created to inform, educate, or influence a specific audience or person. Content may be released in the form of text, image, video, or audio. Blogging is a form of content.

Content Management System (CMS)

A program that manages all of the aspects of creating content. These may include editing, indexing, navigational elements, etc. The best example of a CMS "system" is WordPress, a free and open source website portal. Almost 60% of all websites are created using WordPress.

Conversion Path

The path, or course of actions, a prospect or potential customer will go through to eventually become a lead (customer). These events can include a call to action, lead form, thank you page, downloadable content, and much more.

> *Throughout this book you will see quotes by the "Father of Modern Marketing", Mr. Philip Kotler.*
> *I personally want to thank Mr. Kotler for allowing me to use some of his quotes in this book. If you would like to see and read more about "the guru of marketing", please go to http://www.philkotler.com*

Conversion Rate

The percentage of people who take a desired action, such as filling out a form, registering, signing up for a newsletter, or any activity other than just a visitor browsing a web page. If 10 people visit your website and 5 fill out a form, the conversion rate would be 50%.

Corporate Identity

All symbols, colors, logos, etc., that make up the public image of an organization. This goes hand in hand with your "brand".

Cost Per lead (CPL)

The total cost marketing (you) pays to acquire a lead (customer). It is an important metric to keep track of and it influences your Customer Acquisition Cost (CAC). CPL can be more in larger urban areas as compared to rural areas BUT it also depends on the occupation, services or products and the keywords being used. For example, CPL for an accident attorney in Los Angeles, CA will cost more than the CPL for an electrician promoting to hang a ceiling fan in the small suburbs of Indianapolis, IN.

Cost Per Click (CPC)

An advertising metric that marketers use to determine the amount they will pay for ads based on how many clicks the ad receives. CPC is used most often with Google Adwords and for Facebook ads. A "click" on one of your text ads or your display banner ads represents a visit, or an interaction with your company's product or service offering. Each "click" costs money and can only be justified by a purchase or "conversion".

Crawl or Crawl-ability

Crawling is the process by which "Bots" (Googlebot, Bingbot, etc.,) visit new and updated web pages to be added to the search engine index. Many computers are used daily (computer farms) to fetch (or "crawl") billions of pages on the web. When a bot visits a page, it finds links on the page and adds them to its list of pages to crawl.

Customer Relationship Management (CRM)

Software that helps you organize all of your marketing and sales activities, leads, and more. a good CRM software will include storing contact information, tracking emails, storing deals, and more.

Customer Success Manager/Management (CSM)

In business, it is all about the customer. A CSM is a program developed that allows you or your sales/customer representative to put the customer first. A customer success manager guides customers through the sales process into the support phase and throughout the whole process. In electrical terms, this may be you informing the customer at every step what is going on with the job. From permit pull to job initiation and from job finalization through final inspection.

Customer Acquisition Cost (CAC)

A measurement that allows you to assess the cost of acquiring a new customer and scaling up your business. It can be calculated by dividing the time and money spent on customer acquisition for a specific period of time by the number of new customers gained. (Money + Time Spent)/Number of New Customers. For example, if your company spent $10,000 on marketing in a year and acquired 10,000 customers in the same year, their CAC is $1.00 per new customer.

Customer Loyalty

When a consumer is a repeat buyer of a product, service or brand. These are the customers that you want in every aspect of your electrical business.

Deal Closing

Just as when you "closed the deal" on a new house, a prospect (potential customer) agrees to purchase a product or service and completes a sales transaction thus becoming a conversion.

Decision-Maker

The person in a position to make the final choice about or about buying a product or service.

Demographics

A specific profiling aspect that takes into consideration location, age, gender, income, family life, social class, etc. It's often used in segmentation or for focal points in marketing and advertising strategies. Demographics can be highly useful when sending print or digital media or direct mail to targets.

Digital Marketing (Online Marketing)

Marketing to a target audience solely via the internet. Could be email (eBlast) marketing, content marketing, etc.

Direct Competition

Competitors (for small electricians, usually very local) that provide the exact same services as your company.

Direct Mail

A means of print-on-paper advertising communication that reaches a consumer where they live or their place of business, through the mail, often based on demographics and/or geographical location. See EDDM™ marketing.

Direct Marketing (Direct Response Marketing)

Dealing Directly with the 'end user' rather than a third party or a middle man. Also can be seen as directly communicating with your primary target audience. Can come in the form of advertising, marketing or communications. Some direct online marketing can be considered "spam" and has led to spam laws.

Discovery Call

The very first call with a prospect or potential customer. The purpose is to find out if they're a good fit to work with your organization or if you are a good fit to work for their organization.

Discovery Forms or Papers

If you are dealing with a marketing agency, these will be the papers that you fill out to help lead the agency in the right path to help you achieve your marketing goals.

Domain

To be simplistic, a domain name is your website name. Think of a domain name as an address where Internet users can access your website. The following is a domain: www.powersurgeseo.com. This domain points to my company's website.

Ebook

Also referred to as a lead magnet, ebooks are usually a piece of longer content designed to generate leads. In simpler terms, eBooks are files that you can read on a digital device – a tablet, smartphone, computer, etc.

E-Commerce

The means of selling products digitally on the internet. Amazon is an eCommerce site.

EDDM™ (Every Door Direct Mailer™)

EDDM© is a program sponsored by the United States Postal Service (USPS) allowing regular individuals to mass mail out postcards or direct mail to specific zip codes of your choosing. This allows for a more targeted direct mail campaign for your business. There is a section devoted to EDDM™ later in this book.

Email

A digital message you can send through the internet to contacts, leads and prospects. Online marketing through email allows a businesses direct access into a consumer's inbox and provides the ability to create a connection and build trust.

Engagement

Keeping prospects and customers interested in your brand and invested in your success with the understanding that it's to their benefit, as well. Typically customers like engagement marketing because it encourages them to participate in the evolution of a product, a brand or a brand experience. In a sense, they feel "needed" or "necessary" to the brand.

Engagement Rate

A measurement of likes, shares, comments or other interaction a particular piece of content receives. If you have ever hit the "like" button, you have engaged.

Forecasting

A prediction of marketing and sales trends that are likely to occur in the near or distant future. This forecast is based on historical, quantitative, and qualitative data.

Friction

Any aspect of your website that is hard to understand, distracting or causes visitors to move on from your page. Friction can be as simple as a slow-loading website.

Funnel

A funnel is a strategic way of tracking how your marketing guides potential customers throughout the buying process.

Top of the Funnel (TOFU)

Whereas Bottom of the Funnel (BOFU) prospects are in the ready-to-buy stage, TOFU customers are at the initial stages of the buying process. They are looking for answers to a problem they just realized they are having. Marketers create TOFU content that help prospects identify the problem and leads them to solutions.

Middle of the Funnel (MOFU)

The stage of the sales funnel in which a potential buyer or customer enters after they have identified a problem. This is the point at which you position your business as the solution to their problem.

Bottom of the Funnel

A stage in the buying process, this happens last, when leads move through the top of the funnel (awareness – identifying a problem), the middle (interest and consideration – shopping for solutions), and finally, to the bottom (evaluation and purchase), where they're ready to buy. At this stage, leads are ready to purchase, interested in a demo, a call, or a free consultation.

Awareness

Interest

Consideration

Intent

Evaulation

Purchase

Googlebot

Googlebot is the web crawler software used by Google, which collects documents from the web to build a searchable index for the Google Search engine.

Google Maps Listing (GML)

Google Map Listings (GML) allows businesses to claim and optimize their listings, encourage reviews, and post articles through the Google My Business dashboard.

Google My Business (GMB)

Google My Business (GMB) is a free and easy-to-use tool for businesses and organizations to manage their online presence across Google, including Search and Maps.

Hashtag

A single word or keyword phrase, written without spaces, with a # in front of it. It allows you and your audience to interact and converse about specific topics on social media.

HTML

Short for HyperText Markup Language or code. This language is the core to websites. Every website uses HTML. The picture on the next page is an example of HTML code. (see also "JavaScript" and image on next page)

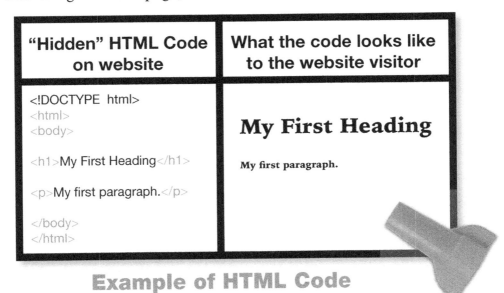

"Hidden" HTML Code on website	What the code looks like to the website visitor

`<!DOCTYPE html>`
`<html>`
`<body>`
 	
`<h1>`My First Heading`</h1>`
 	
`<p>`My first paragraph.`</p>`
 	
`</body>`
`</html>`
	My First Heading
	
	My first paragraph.

Example of HTML Code

Hyperlink (or Link)

A hyperlink is a link from a hypertext file or document to another location or file, typically activated by clicking on a highlighted word or image on the screen. When you see "Click Me", this is an example of a hyperlink.

Ideal Customer Profile (ICP)

The type of customer who meets all the criteria you're looking for in a prospect. In other words, your perfect client.

Inbound Marketing

Advertising your company via content marketing, podcasts, video, eBooks, email broadcast, Social Marketing, etc., rather than paid advertising. Inbound marketing refers to marketing activities that draw visitors in, rather than marketers having to go out to get prospects' attention.

Inbound Links

An inbound link is a link coming from another site to your own website and used rather extensively in organic SEO. Inbound links can be considered citations that refer visitors from one site to another.

Index or Indexing

In simple terms, indexing is the process of adding web pages into Google search or the actions performed by a search engine like Google. Depending upon which meta tag(s) you used, a search engine will crawl and index your pages. A no-index tag means that the page will not be added to the web search's index. By default, every WordPress post and page is indexed.

Infographic

A type of content that is visual in nature, making complex information easy to understand and digest. This is one explanation why children's books have so many pictures in them making them more understandable.

Influencer

In Social Media, Influencers are people that have built a reputation for their fame, knowledge or expertise on a particular topic. They make regular posts about that topic and are usually followed by thousands or millions of fans.

Internet of Things (IOT)

The Internet of Things is basically everything that is involved on the internet. It is a system of interrelated computing devices, mechanical and digital machines provided with unique identifiers and the ability to transfer data over a network without requiring human-to-human or human-to-computer interaction. Nowadays, people can connect almost anything and everything to the internet; dog collars, car finders, dating apps, sobriety tests, smart toasters, and more.

Internet of Things Image by Tumisu from Pixabay

JavaScript

A programming language that lets web developers design interactive sites. Whenever you see "stuff" moving around on a website, chances are it's javaScript based. JavaScript is used to create pop-ups, slide-in calls-to-action, security password creation, check forms, interactive games, and much more. JavaScript is also used to build mobile apps and create server-based applications. The image below is javaScript. It looks very similar to HTML code but is vastly different. HTML is a different type of computer language that consist of various types of elements to represent different forms of data to be displayed on web pages whereas JavaScript is a scripting language to make the static HTML content as dynamic. Usually when you see a website page that is "moving" around, it is javaScript that is allowing that to happen.

Keyword

A specific word or phrase that describes the content of a webpage typically used in an organic SEO campaign. It should always align with your target audience. Below you will see the difference between Long-Tail Keywords and Short-Tail Keywords.

Long-Tail Keyword

A long-tail keyword is a very targeted search phrase that contains three or more words. It often contains a head term plus one or two additional words that refine the search term.

For example:
- Head term: *electrician*
- Long-tail keywords: *electrician specializing in automation and controls, electrician replace mast heads, electrician on YouTube, etc.,*

Long-tail keywords are more specific, which means visitors that land on your website from a long-tail search term are more likely to hire you for your services. Short-tail keywords have a higher search rate but lower conversion. Long-tail keywords have a lower search rate but higher conversion.

Short-Tail Keyword

Short-tail keywords are search phrases with only one or two words. Their length makes them less specific than searches with more words. "Electrician" (1 word) or "Atlanta Electrician" (2 words) is an example of a short-tail keyword, whereas "Electricians specializing in automation and controls" (6 words) is a long-tail keyword. Short-tail keywords have a higher search rate but lower conversion. Long-tail keywords have a lower search rate but higher conversion.

Key Performance Indicator (KPI)

A means to measure the performance of various factors, from employee functions to marketing tactics. Tracking KPIs will help your organization achieve its goals. An example of a KPI is your company's profit and loss (P&L) statement. KPIs are used to check the performance of your marketing.

Landing Page

A page on your website that houses a form that prospects will fill out and exchange their personal information for a something in return such as a lead magnet or free offer (ebook, demo, consultation, etc.).

Lead

An individual or a company that has shown interest in one of your products or services.

Lead generation

Activities with the purpose of generating interest about your product or service. These activities may include content marketing, blogging, advertising, enticements, referrals and partnerships.

Lead Nurturing

Engaging and building relationships with potential customers through a variety of marketing techniques in hopes that they will soon become a paying customer.

Lead Qualification

A method of determination of whether a client fits your organization's vision of the ideal customer.

Lifetime Customer Value

A prediction of the net profit attributed to the entire future relationship with a customer.

Link (see Hyperlink)

Link Wheel (See illustration on next page)

A link wheel is a circular approach to create links between high quality websites of various types that also link to your website. The link wheel is where several similar themed websites join together to create a circle of links. **For example, "your" electrical website A links to electrical magazine website B which links to electrical parts website C which then links back to "your" electrical website A.** Link wheels can contain any number of websites from the three in this example upwards.

Local Service Ads (See illustration on next page)

A pay-per-lead service provided by Google. This service was originally called "Google Home Services" before being rebranded. Although a service for all businesses, Local Service Ads has not yet been instituted in every US city.

Loss Aversion

Refers to the psychological idea that people feel more negative about losing money than they do about the prospect of gaining "equivalent" money.

LSI Keywords

Latent Semantic Indexing (LSI) keywords are words that are commonly found together within a single topic and are semantically related to each other. In the case of electricians, LSI keywords will be receptacle, wire, voltage, panel, wire nut, etc.,

Margin

The profit gained from a product or service after all of the expenses for selling that product or service are covered.

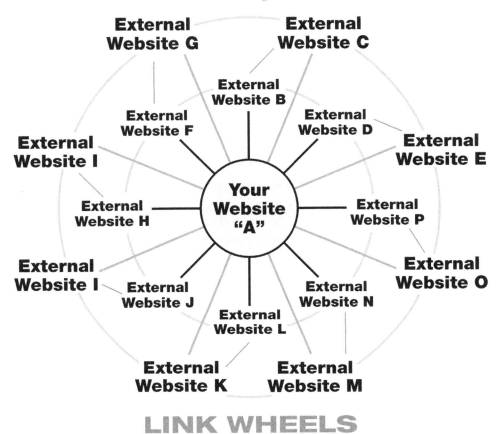

LINK WHEELS

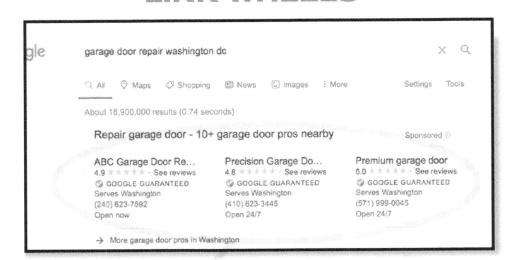

Example of Google Local Service Ads

Marketing Automation

This is the tool that lets you "automate" your marketing campaigns. Through lead nurturing, behavior-based strategies and more, you can use marketing automation to send the right marketing messages to the right people at the right time. Think "GoHighlevel" software (https://www.gohighlevel.com).

Market Penetration

A strategy used to sell more of an existing product within the current markets it is being sold. As an electrician, you may offer substantial discounts to a specific demographic to acquire more market share so as to be more competitive.

Market Research

High-intelligence research and development of a specific industry for the betterment of sound business decisions.

Marketing

The process of identifying, anticipating and satisfying customer requirements in a profitable way for you and a beneficial way for your customer.

Marketing Pixel (see Pixel)

Meta Description

When you perform a Google search for a product, service, company, etc., the meta description can be found to describe the product, service, company, etc.

Meta Tags

Meta Tags are snippets of text that describe a page's content; the Meta Tags don't appear on the page itself, but only in the page's source code. Meta Tags are essentially little content descriptors that help tell search engines what a web page is about.

Here are some examples of Meta Tags in the electrical industry.

Title Meta Tag

"Healthcare Electrician & Electrical Contractors | Atlanta | Covington"

Description Meta Tag

"When it comes to healthcare electrical services, John Doe Electrical Contractors has the knowledge and the manpower to get the job done."

 ozburnelectrical.com

Electrician Near Me | Electrical Contractors | Covington | Atlanta

Ozburn Electrical Contractors when it comes to high quality electrical work. Metro Atlanta, GA's best electricians ready to service your electrical needs.

An example of Meta Descriptions; here the small snippet of text that best describes your page's content on the SERP.

Monthly Recurring Revenue

The amount of income produced each month from subscriptions to your products or services. This may be considered residual income.

NAP (Name, Address, Phone)

It's critical when listing your website among directories that you have your Name, Address and Phone number consistent from directory site to directory site. We will talk more about this in the "online directories" portion of this book.

Niche Market/Business

A very specific segment of a market in which you are trying to meet the needs of that market. This book is trying to meet the marketing needs for the electrical niche.

Onboarding (aka Customer Onboarding)

This term can refer to introducing a new customer or client to your services or products, or it's used to describe assimilating a new employee into your organization. Onboarding can also be the initial process of compiling necessary information from your customer to your business.

Offer

This is an asset, tangible or intangible, that you'll offer prospects on a landing page. The offer is designed to help you generate leads or customers, and they can include everything from a webinar, ebook, checklist, template, demo and more.

"Organic" Listing (On-Page, Off-Page SEO)

A 'search engine organic listing' refers to the natural or unpaid listing of a website on a SERP or search result page. Organic listings are natural "organic" listings of web pages that Google has crawled, indexed, and deemed valuable for the search term used by the searcher. The more informative and valuable the page around a key term, the higher it is ranked. This is one reason why on-page and off-page SEO is so important in your marketing plan.

"Organic" Search

Organic search is a method for entering one or several search terms as a single string of text into a search engine. On-Page SEO is organically driven. Organic search results appear based on relevance to the search term or terms, and exclude paid advertisements; whereas non-organic search (PPC) results do not filter out pay-per-click advertising. Organic is as the word's meaning of having the characteristics of an organism. An organism, such as a plant or animal, grows over time. Organic search results are not "paid" search results. Organic search results "grow over time" based on the amount of on-page and off-page SEO dedicated to a website. See "Pay-Per-Click".

Over the Top (OTT)

iMessage, Whatsapp, WeChat, Facebook Messenger, and other messaging applications are often referred to as "Over The Top" (OTT) applications.

Paid Listings

Also known as pay-per-click, (Paid Google listings; also known as Adwords), or other nicknames are paid positions within a search engine like Google. An advertiser (your electrical company) positions their ad in this section of the search listings and are charged (by Google) every time someone clicks on the ad.

P&L Statement

A financial statement that summarizes the revenues, costs, and expenses incurred during a specified period, usually a fiscal quarter or year.

Pay-Per-Click (PPC)

A method of advertising on the internet where you only pay when someone "clicks" on your ad. This is common with Facebook and Google paid marketing. PPC is the opposite of organic growth known as SEO. See "Organic".

Pixel or Marketing Pixel

Marketing pixels, also know as tracking pixels, are essentially these tiny snippets of code that allow a website owner, business, marketer or advertiser to gather information about visitors on a website. Once the visitor visits the website, their information is embedded with this code that allows for Retargeting Ads. This explains when you are shopping for shoes and then everywhere you look, there is a shoe ad. For example, The Facebook pixel is a small piece of code that goes on your website. With this "pixel", you can trace or follow website visitors, or find new people who will likely make a purchase or become a lead.

Podcast

A podcast is an audio program that is comprised up of a series of spoken word that focus on a particular topic or theme. An example of a podcast would be if you, an electrician, wanted to do a weekly recorded audio conversation with electrical supply manufacturers. You can then syndicate your "podcast" as if you were on radio.

Point Of Contact (POC)

The representative who is the decision maker/facilitator for an organization.

Portfolio

A series of case studies that provide proof of value and expertise to potential customers.

Press Release (PR)

A press release is a short, compelling official statement delivered to members of the news media for the purpose of providing information, a product launch, an official statement, or making an announcement. Press releases are an excellent way to create a citation for your business. *My company offers Press Releases as an excellent source of a citation for your website.*

Public Relations (PR)

A series of media releases, press releases, conferences, social images, etc. that make up and maintain the reputation of an organization and its brands.

QR Code

Developed by Toyota, a QR Code (Quick Response) is a type of matrix barcode. In marketing , QR codes can quickly lead a viewer, via smart device, to a predetermine location.

This is an example of a QR code. *Hold your smartphone's camera over the code and a link should appear. Click the link and you will be taken to a location.*

Qualified Lead

A lead that is qualified meets your company's criteria, or buyer attributes, and is more likely to make a purchase.

Research and Development (R&D)

The process of discovering and developing new products and services.

Responsive Design

A website that changes based on the device the consumer uses. Mobile, laptop, and desktop devices offer different views of a website, and responsive design accommodate for each view, without having to build separate websites for each one. Responsive designs are necessary because of the new Google Algorithms that place more emphasis on mobile responsiveness.

Return On Investment (ROI)

A way to measure the profitability of the investment you make. If the ROI on an investment is negative, it generally means you're losing money on that endeavor. Measuring the ROI on your marketing budget can give you a better sense of how to adapt your market to future changes.

Referral

A prospect or lead generated from someone who may be interested in what the salesperson is selling.

Relationship Marketing

Similar to engagement, relationship marketing is the intent of developing a long term association with a prospect or potential customer. This strategy is much less expensive than gaining new customers.

Repeat & Referral

A prospect or lead generated from someone who has spoken highly of your company to someone who may be interested in finding your products and services. Generating repeat customers and referrals is the most effective, affordable way to build your business.

ReCAPTCHA

reCAPTCHA is a free service from Google that helps protect websites from robots, spam and similar other abuse. A "CAPTCHA" is a test to tell humans apart from "bots" or robots. It is usually easy for humans to solve, but hard for "bots" and other malicious software to figure out. (Sometimes hard for us humans to figure out!)

Retargeting

Retargeting is a form of online targeted advertising by which your actions are "followed" by online advertisers based on your previous internet actions. Retargeting "tags" online users by including a pixel within the target webpage or email, which sets a cookie in the user's browser.

Sales Funnel (See Funnel)

The entire sales process as a whole – from prospect to paying customer – and all marketing, advertising and sales processes in between.

Schema Markup

Schema markup is code that is put on your website to help ensure the search engines return more informative results for users.

Search Engine Optimization (SEO)

An "organic" method to increase a webpage's performance in web search results. By tweaking elements on the website itself (on-page SEO) and off-page SEO factors, you can move a webpage up on a search result "page". SEO elements include keywords, title and image tags, links, and more.

On-Page Optimization (On-Page SEO)

This type of SEO is based solely on a webpage and the various elements within the HTML. On-Page ensures that key pieces of the specific page (content, title tag, URL, and image tags) include the desired keyword(s) that will help a page rank higher for that particular keyword or phrase.

Off-Page Optimization (Off-Page SEO)

Off-page SEO is not performed on the website itself, but rather as a compliment to On-Page SEO optimization. Off-Page optimization refers to creating incoming links and other outside factors, including directories and citations, that impact how a webpage is indexed in search results. Many factors, including linking domains and social media pages, play a role in Off-Page optimization. The good news is that it's powerful and less expensive than pay-per-click (PPC). The bad news is that the results are mostly out of an inbound marketer's control and it takes time to build up your website's authority. Their are creative "work arounds" to the "bad news" such as, you can create useful, remarkable content (blogging, etc.,) and chances are people will share and link to it.

Organic SEO

Organic search engine optimization (organic SEO) refers to the methods used to obtain a higher SERP placement (or ranking) using unpaid, algorithm-driven results on a given search engine such as Google, Yahoo, Bing, and more. Marketer methods such as boosting keywords, backlinks and writing high-quality content can significantly improve a site's page rank. Backlinks are especially valuable for SEO because they represent a "vote of confidence" from one site to another. In essence, manually listed backlinks (directories, citations, other websites, other blogs etc.,) to your website are a signal to search engines that others sites vouch for your content and also your website. Sites using organic SEO will be much like the root word, organisms, meaning they will grow, expand and adapt over time in response to readers' desires. Organic SEO is less expensive than PPC but the results may be slower whereas PPC has almost instant results, but is much more expensive.

Search Engine Results Page (SERP)

SERP is the search result pages after someone has performed a query in a search engine such as Google or Bing. Marketers generally want to get their website page to appear on page 1 of a search result, ideally at the very top of the page.

Social Media

Social media is media designed to be shared through online social interaction, created using platforms like Facebook, Twitter, LinkedIn, Instagram and Snapchat that help users connect. Marketers use these networks to increase awareness, grow their customer base and achieve business goals.

Software-as-a-Service (SaaS)

Any software (e.g. Con-Est, Procore, Service Titan, Rakken, Housecall Pro, etc.,) that is hosted by another company, which stores your information in the cloud.

SMS

SMS stands for Short Message Service that are limited to 160 characters. It is known as one of the oldest texting technologies. This is probably what you use to "text" your friends and family.

Text "Electrician" to 85679 for $25 off your next service".

To stop receiving messages, reply "STOP". For help, reply "HELP". Msg & data rates may apply.

Electrician

S.W.O.T. Analysis (Strengths, Weaknesses, Opportunities and Threats)

An internal study often used by organizations to identify their strengths, weaknesses, opportunities and threats.

Target Marketing

A group of customers toward which a business has decided to aim its marketing efforts and merchandise. As an electrician, you may target residential, commercial or industrial targets with a focus on a particular segment of your services. For example, if you may target Industrial Engineers with PLC knowledge or Automation and Controls services.

Text Messaging (SMS)

SMS is a text messaging service component of most telephone, Internet, and mobile device systems. SMS uses protocols to enable mobile devices to exchange short text messages. An example would be like "text 'electrician' to 85679 for $25 off your next service". See also SMS.

Unique Selling Proposition

The "unique selling proposition" is the factor that differentiates your products and services from your competitors, such as the low cost, warranty, the quality, 24/7, etc.

URL

This is short for Uniform Resource Locator or basically your domain such as https://www.electricalbusiness.com. The URL is very important to a successful marketing campaign. Every page of a website has it's own separate URL.

User Experience

The experience a user has with your brand/website, from the moment they discover you, through the visit, acceptance of a/the need of your products and services, purchase and beyond. This is where customers can become your strongest advocates.

Value Statement

A description of your company's top priorities and how those translate into marketing and sales initiatives. A "value statement" usually states how you "value" your customer.

Viral Marketing

A method of marketing that encourages the viewer to share or help promote an idea, product or service on their own. An example of "viral marketing" would be for you to promote your electrical business via a great coupon. This coupon is so great that everyone has to share with others. This is viral marketing at its simplest form.

Volume

Keyword search volume refers to the volume (or number) of searches for a particular keyword in a given timeframe. The search volume is usually an average over a set period of time to provide marketers and agencies with a general idea of a keyword's search term competitiveness.

Webinar

The word "webinar" is a combination of "Web" and "Seminar" and is pretty much what it stands for. It is a video workshop, lecture, or presentation hosted online using webinar software such as Zoom, Google Meet, and more.

Website

A series of webpages that are connected, beginning with a homepage and generally includes other pages like "contact," "about," "services" and more. As an electrical company serving many individuals or organizations, your website should be strategically designed to attract visitors, convert users into leads and then turn leads into customers.

WordPress (WP)

WordPress is a free and open-source content management system (CMS). WP is used by more than 60 million websites, including 33.6% of the top 10 million websites as of April 2019, WordPress is one of the most popular content management system solutions in use. See "Content Management Systems".

Workflow

A series of emails, similar to "funnels", that are designed to nurture leads. A powerful marketing asset, you can use workflows to engage leads, learn more about prospects, segment lists, and much more.

Know of any other words not listed? You can list them here for your own personal record.

_____

_____

_____

_____

_____

_____

_____

_____

_____

_____

POWER SURGE SEO

Call us today at
1-888-235-4SEO(4736)
www.PowerSurgeSEO.com
help@www.PowerSurgeSEO.com

Notes

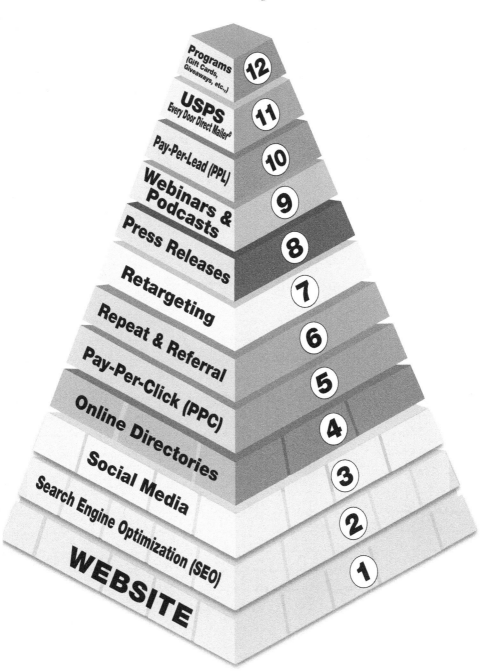

Pyramid of Marketing Success

Pyramid of Marketing Success

First and most importantly, do you already have a website or do you need to design or create a website? If you already have a website, you need to check the "look and feel" of it to make sure that the branding is what you want from this day forward. Do you remember earlier (p. 18) when I mentioned "foundation"? We need your website to be the core foundation of your marketing plan. Your website will now become the "base of operations", "the command post", per se. From this day forward, the majority of your online marketing will be based on your website as the foundation and just like any "command post", it needs to have a solid foundation and be fortified. Each level of the marketing pyramid will essentially be an offshoot of your website.

Let's take a look at each level of the *"Pyramid of Marketing Success"* and see how we can incorporate elements into your marketing plan, starting with number 1, the website. If at anytime you feel overwhelmed, put this book down and take a break. If you ever need any help, you can always rely on us at *help@powersurgeseo.com.*

1) The Website (aka The Foundation)

A solid foundation is necessary for any successful online marketing plan. Earlier I stated that 97% of consumers go online to find and research local products and services. When those 97% perform a "Google Search"for an electrician, where do you think it should lead them to? Your website of course! A website can add to your business in many ways by adding a professional look and validation to your company. It also provides ease of access to your products and services and provides, at least, an even playing field

> *"Every business is a service business. You are not a chemical company. You are a chemical services business."*
> — **Philip Kotler**

between you and your competition. In the long run, a website will be your least expensive marketing tool that will provide a large impact on your business. In a sense, a website will give you the best "return on investment".

Historically, having a website, next to paid ads, is the most cost effective marketing method when looking at cost per 1,000 impressions. Your website will be much more effective though than paid ads, provided by Facebook or Google, because people who visit and see your website are actively engaged in learning more about your company, products and services. Having people actively engaged on your website will most likely result in many more leads converting to customers in the long run.

Also, we will be using my brother's (and customer) real live electrical company, Ozburn Electrical Contractors, Inc. as an example throughout this book. **It's easier to ask for forgiveness** from my brother, Terry Ozburn, **rather than asking for permission** (just joking). Plus, it's free advertising for his company.

You can see his website at www.OzburnElectrical.com

Whenever I mention "Ozburn Electrical Contractors, Inc.", please substitute your business's name in place of it to have a better understanding of how a marketing strategy can help you and your business.

2) SEO, Search Engine Optimization

I cannot impress on you enough the importance of the second level (#2) of the marketing pyramid, <u>a good SEO plan</u>. When you think of SEO, in my opinion, it is the equivalent of having an excellent accountant. For those of you who know the importance of having a great accountant, you can appreciate the analogy. However much money that you spend on a good, solid SEO plan, it will most likely payoff in many ways in the future. Good SEO is certainly an investment, but it can, and should, pay for itself when done correctly. SEO is also known as an "organic search" strategy as opposed to PPC's "pay as you go" strategy. Today, SEO still remains the dominant source of trackable web traffic with an average traffic share of 53% across industries. You'd think the importance of organic traffic from search engines would make investing in SEO a no-brainer, but marketers and business owners often have real concerns about incorporating SEO into their overall strategy. **From my experience, SEO works!** It may take a few months to get going, but it works. I will explain my "80/20" rule later in this book (pp. 71-72). Try to incorporate this rule into your SEO vs. PPC marketing budget and I am sure you will get good results.

Earlier I stated that 97% of consumers go online to find and research local products and services. When those 97% perform a "Google Search", hopefully your sound SEO marketing plan, based on the proper keywords, meta descriptions, meta tags, and back links, will lead them to your website or at least your Google My Business page. Over time, a properly instituted SEO plan helps small business websites rank higher in search engines results, which in turn helps bring more qualified potential leads, or customers, to your site that eventually turn into phone calls that increase your conversion rates and sales.

SEO (Search Engine Optimization), which is making sure that your site is optimized to show up in your organic listing when someone types (Google, Bing, Yahoo, Baidu, etc.,) in the search bar the key words that are important to your success as an electrician. Your goal for your company is to be found on the first page of a local search results page (SERP).

"Google tells us that 92% of searchers will pick businesses on the first page of local search results."

There is "on-site SEO" and "off-site SEO". On-site SEO (also referred to as on-page SEO) is the practice of optimizing elements on a website (as opposed to links elsewhere on the Internet and other external signals collectively known as "off-site SEO").

On-site SEO is preformed in order to rank higher and earn more relevant traffic from search engines. When I mentioned "foundation" earlier, this is one of the key strategies that I was referring to. This is a cornerstone element that needs to be added and performed at the initial stages of your website. Don't worry if you already have a website built. You can apply on-site SEO after the fact but it is so much easier to do it at the beginning of a new, fresh website build.

For example, if wiring your own new house from "ground up", would you take the time to do a little extra and add a few more receptacles and a few more can lights than called for? Since this is your home, you will tend to embellish the electrical schematics a little. Same with your website. On-site SEO is just one of those moments to "embellish" the meta tags, code and etc., that tell search engines, such as Google and Bing, important information about your web page, such as how they should display it in the search results.

These "organic" search result pages are called "Search Engine Results Pages" (SERP). These are the pages displayed by search engines in response to a query by a user. A well devised "on-site SEO" could possibly, even on it's own, eventually lead to conversions or "sales". Conversions are what you want to achieve from your website. SEO, through a "search", resonates with the customer that's looking for your electrical services, so that they pick up the phone and call you as opposed to hitting the back button and searching around.

Whenever you see the use of the term "Google" in this book, in most cases I am referring to Google but it covers all search engines such as "Bing", "Yahoo", "Duck Duck Go", and more.

SEO not only helps build brand awareness for your business, more leads or potential customers are likely to trust a site that lands on the first page of search engine results pages (SERPs) than companies who are not utilizing SEO.

Here's a question. After you performed a Google "search" for a company, service or product, how many pages of the SERP do you flip through? **The first page and maybe the second and if you really are interested, the third page?** Most consumers will look at the first and second page results from the search results pages and stop there. *Do you want your electrical company to be on the Google page 3 search results?* After reading this book, I hope you are empowered enough to be able to hire the right people to perform your on-page and off-page SEO.

Most likely if you are reading this book, you are either a small business owner or thinking about owning your own business. If so, you should adopt a SEO strategy early, to build a strong web presence and bypass your competition. In some cases, it may be better just to start over and rebuild your website to give it a fresh start with the on-page SEO. If you are talking to a marketing professional and they suggest a new website, don't be alarmed. Most likely this is not the marketing agency trying to make more money off of you but rather they feel that you would be better served with a new beginning. SEO is hard work but it can be much harder if you have to correct what others have done so that you can properly institute a base for on-page SEO.

In the long run, this will help you gain new customers for your electrical business and hopefully take it to the next level.

3) Social Media

The third level (#3) of the pyramid is "Social Media". Social Media, for both a small or large electrical business, can feel overwhelming and challenging if you, as a business owner, are doing it yourself. If you are in business "start-up" mode, it may be crucial for you to initially take on more of the marketing duties. As your business grows, you can eventually turn marketing duties over to a trusted work associate or even to a marketing agency.

Feel free to contact our marketing agency, Power Surge SEO, if you have any questions. **We can easily be reached at help@power-surgeseo.com or 1-888-235-4SEO (4736).**

Social media does make spreading the word about your electrical contracting business faster and easier. By having an active social media presence, you can immediately start building relationships with your audience, leads and customers.

In the initial stages of marketing your business, when it comes to managing your own social media, less is more. Pick one or two social networks and focus on quality over quantity. If you are an electrician that wants to solely focus on residential electrical service, try creating a Facebook business page and/or an Instagram page. If you are an electrician that wants to concentrate more on commercial, retail or industrial, try Facebook and LinkedIn. Linke-dIn allows you to connect with industry leaders in your local area. These leaders may be looking for a specialist in automation and controls, PLCs, VFDs, and more. It would make sense to post articles and messages that promote your commercial or industrial electrical business using LinkedIn. Not only are industry leaders using LinkedIn, plant managers, engineers, plant maintenance foremen, and more use it to keep informed and to keep all of their employment options open. Nevertheless, all social media is a way to promote your business effectively, efficiently, and most importantly, inexpensively.

> *Please note that Facebook Ads play a vital and important role in today's advertising strategies. If you plan on the majority of your electrical services devoted to residential work, FB Ads are vital. This book is more about how to effectively market your business via organic (SEO, Blogging, Citations, etc.,) whereas FB Ads fall under the PPC category. In the future, I plan on writing another book that specifically details more about pay-per-click ads. See more about PPC on page 71.*

4) Online Directories

The fourth level, "Online Directories", can also be considered "Citations". I mentioned this because it is important to note the verbiage when and if you are doing your own research or if you have hired a marketing agency. ***Please also keep in mind that every directory listing is a citation, but not every citation is a directory listing.*** Remember that citations are any web post(s) that mentions or "cites" your company. Typically, a directory site will mention your company more frequently but it can be a written article, a press release, and more. In simple terms, citations are important. Citations, when listed properly, mention your company around the web. These mentions are not link based by any means. They are purely textual mentions of a company along with its (NAP) or company name, physical address and phone number.

With citations, you must make sure that your business name is listed *exactly* like you want it consistently represented across the internet. It all starts again at the "foundation" of your website. Citations help Google's "ever changing" algorithm to determine if your company is real, fake, permanently closed, and more.

> *"Keep in mind that every Directory Listing is a Citation, but not every Citation is a Directory Listing."*
> *- Confucius*

Directories (and/or Citations) - You may be already using the services of some of the top online directories. Not surprising is the fact that Google is the #1 online directory. You may be surprised to find that YouTube (owned by Google) is also considered a directory and comes in as the #2 directory that consumers find themselves searching for information, products and services.
(FYI *-people love relatively short and to the point videos*)

Here is the short list, according to Alexa.com of the top sites (including directories) in the United States as of late 2020.

1) Google.com
2) Youtube.com
3) Amazon.com
4) Yahoo.com
5) Facebook.com
6) Reddit.com
7) Zoom.us
8) Wikipedia.org
9) Myshopify.com
10) Ebay.com

Most of you have heard of few of the most common Online Directories. These are more commonly considered directories because they typically define themselves as directories. **Here is the short list of defined directories in 2020, according to Whitespark.ca.**

1) Google My Business
2) Apple Maps
3) Foursquare
4) Bing Places
5) Yelp
6) TomTom
7) Yellowpages (online)
8) Infogroup
9) LocalEze
10) Factual

If your company is a member of Dun & Bradstreet, Better Business Bureau or the Chamber of Commerce, you're part of a directory. These board or trade websites are also considered directory sites. Please check the Appendix in the back of this book for more information about Directories.

Earlier in this book on pp. 22-23, I had you fill out some business information. At the beginning, I had you list your business's legal name, common name, and "slang" names or names other than what you typically call your business. I asked those questions, not for my sake, but for your sake. I want you to know your business's nomenclature so that you would be able to comfortably setup "citations" or at least assist your marketing agency of exactly how you want your name to be across the web.

This picture represents just one example of how to setup citations for your electrical business. First, start with your electrical business's webpage

I will be using www.OzburnElectrical.com as an example.
If you noticed, although the website is OzburnElectrical.com, I have prominently put the actual name, Ozburn Electrical Contractors, Inc., at the top of the home page. Most see it as just a header that tells the name of the company and that would be correct but in SEO language, this is part of our "on-site SEO" plan that will help with Google's algorithm when matching "citations" (your legal or

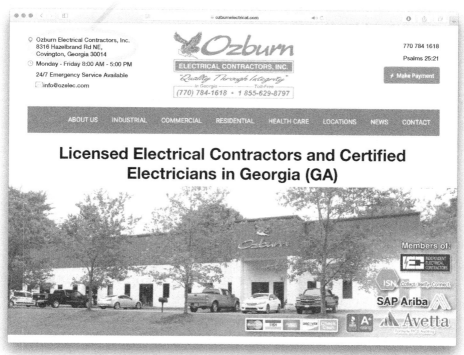

common business name) that are mentioned at specific locations (directories) across the web. You need to make sure that, throughout your website, you include your name and consistently match the exact spelling and nomenclature of the name itself so that it is consistent across the internet from citation to citation (from sea to shining sea). When Google or another search engine sees consistency, it creates trust from Google in helping to determine if your site is not only a trust-worthy site, but also a viable, fluid site that represents an actual electrical company. This is extremely important when listing citations among the many directories that are on the internet.

Let's say that your business name is "Atlanta Electrical Services". My marketing advice to you (not all marketers succeed in this) is to keep your name consistent as "Atlanta Electrical Services" when creating citations (Directories...aka: Yelp, Yahoo Local Listings, LinkedIn, etc.,). Here are a few common mistakes some business owner and marketing agencies make when listing citations.

What it should be (legal or common name):
Atlanta Electrical Services

What Google actually sees on the web (slang names):
ATL Electrical Services, Atlanta Electric, Atlanta Electric Services, Atlanta Electric Company, ATL Electrical Contractor, Atlanta Electrical Contractors, and on and on.

You have to remember that Google and other search engines are automated and use some of the most sophisticated algorithms known to man yet Google is "matter of fact" in that is sees a written name and can't determine if other similar names are the same company.

Although brilliantly written software, search engines do not have the sophisticated "human" intellect or ability to recognize that every single "slang" name represents the same company. To Google, all of those slang names could be many different companies with similar names.

This is one reason that it is so important to make sure that your electrical business name is consistent from sea to shining sea or citation to citation. Just keep this in mind if you plan on listing your own business citations or if you are working with an agency.

5) PPC (Pay-Per-Click)

PPC stands for pay-per-click, a model of internet marketing in which advertisers (potentially you) pay a fee each time one of their ads is clicked. Essentially, it's a way of buying visits to your site, rather than attempting to "earn" those visits organically (SEO).

PPC in the long run could be very expensive but if planned correctly in conjunction with a solid SEO plan, it could work well. A lot of marketers like to use a rule in which I call the "80-20" rule. This is where you start a marketing campaign as follows. If you are solely marketing using only SEO and PPC, under this rule, the first month you spend 80% of your budget on PPC and 20% on organic SEO. The second month you would spend 70% on PPC and 30% on SEO. The third month you would spend 60% on PPC and 40% on SEO. You would do this monthly until the seventh month when you should be spending at 20% PPC and 80% SEO.

Using this "see saw" plan, you get immediate ad awareness through PPC while taking a few months to build up a solid SEO game.

80/20 Rule			$500 Budget		$___ Budget	
	PPC	SEO	PPC	SEO	PPC	SEO
Month 1	80%	20%	$400	$100	$_____	$_____
Month 2	70%	30%	$350	$150	$_____	$_____
Month 3	60%	40%	$300	$200	$_____	$_____
Month 4	50%	50%	$250	$250	$_____	$_____
Month 5	40%	60%	$200	$300	$_____	$_____
Month 6	30%	70%	$150	$350	$_____	$_____
Month 7	20%	80%	$100	$400	$_____	$_____

The "80/20 Rule" seen below, is not the *Pareto Principle*, which states that 80% of your sales come from 20% of your customers. This "80/20 Rule" is more for your marketing budget as it applies to spending money on paid ads vs on-page and off-Page SEO that is organically applied to your website. Either way you will end up spending money. PPC is paid Ads with fairly instant results. Once the end result (click, funnel, etc.,) is completed, you have spent your money. SEO applies more to someone using "elbow grease" and manually applying sophisticated techniques on and off your website. This includes back links, meta links, internal and external links and more. Once someone starts the SEO process, it ramps up over the months until you have reached visibility to the searcher. If you turn your monthly SEO off, the results start to ramp back down until you are no longer noticed by the searcher. This may take months to happen whereas PPC is instant.

If a business is new and getting started, I would recommend this plan of attack just to ramp up the business quickly. Once you get established, try to spend more money on the SEO portion. I personally believe that SEO, in the long run, is money well spent.

6) Repeat & Referral

Long before digital files and online marketing and even further back into history, there has been a tried and trued method of getting business. What I am referring to is the Repeat & Referral way of obtaining customers. Not only is it the oldest method that we will talk about, it is probably the least expensive method as well.

Customer Service "Feedback Forms" are always a great way to obtain data from your customers.

Over the years, generating repeat customers and referrals has been the most effective, affordable way to build a business. The costs are very inexpensive to keep a customer and solicit referrals compared

Ozburn Electrical Contractors, Inc.
8316 Hazelbrand Rd NE
Covington, GA 30014
(770) 784-1618
info@ozelec.com
www.OzburnElectrical.com

Date Visited: _____ Lead Electrician's Name: _____

Customer Service Feedback Form

At Ozburn Electric, we are constantly trying to improve the quality of the work we do and we place great importance on the views of our customers. Please help us to improve and develop our services further by completing this brief questionnaire.

Please answer the extent to which you agree or disagree with the following statements:

	Strongly agree	Agree	Neither agree nor disagree	Disagree	Strongly disagree
Did the electrical technician(s) arrive during the prescribe time?					
Our electrical technician(s) attended to you in a friendly and professional manner?					
Our electrical technician(s) attended to your electrical needs promptly?					
Our electrical technician(s) explained everything to you in an educated way?					
Our electrical technician(s) were courteous to you?					
How likely is it that you would recommend Ozburn Electric to a friend or colleague?					

As a customer of Ozburn Electrical Contractors, Inc., we truly appreciate your business. We welcome you to follow us on Facebook, LinkedIn, and Instagram. If you would like to receive our newsletter, please enter your email address below. Also, if you would like to be informed of deals, specials and coupons, enter your phone number below so that we can text you the deals! (message and data rates may apply). Simply reply "STOP" to end or "HELP" for help.

NAME:_____

ADDRESS:_____

SIGNATURE:_____

EMAIL ADDRESS:_____

CONTACT TELEPHONE NUMBER: _____

Please remember to "LIKE" us on Google!

Thank you very much!

You can contact the customer service desk at *info@ozelec.com* or call (770) 784-1618.

An Example of a "Customer Feedback Form".

to other marketing techniques. Furthermore, if you have treated your past and present customers like royalty, these Repeat & Referral customers require less work to convert to a sale because they're already conditioned to like you. That's why all marketing plans should include strategies for encouraging repeat and referral business.

One strategy to generate repeat customers and referrals is through follow-up. Follow-up marketing tactics work by keeping your name in front of your customers, clients and prospects, so when they're in need or know someone in need of your services, your name comes to mind. Some of the strategies for repeat business are to include the customer on an email list. Here are a few more strategies to keep your past and present customers informed.

(A) One strategy to generate repeat customers and referrals is through a follow-up strategy. Follow-up marketing tactics work by keeping your name in front of your customers, clients and prospects, so when they're in need or know someone in need of your services, your name comes to mind. Listed below are some of the strategies for repeat business.

(B) Create a database: Whether you have special software for this (Housecall Pro™, ServiceTitan™, LiveAgent™, etc.,) or just use an excel spreadsheet, make sure you have all of your customers in a database. As the owner of an electrical company, it is imperative that you collect as much data from your customers as you can. Make sure this data includes any important and pertinent information like their name, address, email addresses, phone number and any special notes. You may even want to collect data such as birth dates, anniversaries, and more. if nothing else, It is crucial for you to get the first and last name, phone number and email address for future target emails or "friendly" calls. Instruct your team members to be vigilant in retrieving information from the customer. One way to achieve this is after every job, have the customer fill out a "Customer Service Feedback Forms" as seen in the picture to the right. Also make sure to ask the customer to leave you a good review online. All of this information can be used to your advantage in the future.

(C) Birthdays, Anniversaries and Special Days: Why include this kind of info? It may sound obtrusive but your customers appreciate when you send a birthday card or celebrate their anniversary. It shows you took time to listen to them and were actually interested in getting to know them. Building relationships with your customers matters!

(D) Newsletter: Start a newsletter and stay in touch with your customers. Make sure that your newsletters provide value. Don't make them sound too much like a sales promotion. Let them know about new blog posts you posted, new products or services you are offering, or tips of the trade. Be consistent and stay on top of this. Sending an email that contains a weekly or biweekly newsletter keeps your name in their inbox and keeps your business on their minds.

(E) Ask for reviews and testimonials: Create a testimonial form (a short questionnaire) similar to the "Customer Service Feedback Form". Have your customers fill it out when you have completed the sale or service and while the technician is still "loading up the truck". If you have a website and post testimonials/reviews, ask your customers if they are okay with their testimonial being posted onto your website. (if they have their own business they may love it if you add their business name and link under the testimonial) If you do not have this on your website you can always ask them to leave a review on sites like Google My Business (GMB), Yelp, Facebook and LinkedIn. Happy customers love leaving great reviews! **(Warning, Google and most other review sites state in their terms of service that paying for reviews is strictly prohibited and considered illegal. Google, like most review sites, does not allow the**

use of money, discounts, gifts, or other rewards for reviews.)

Warning, Google and most other review sites state in their terms of service that paying for reviews is strictly prohibited and considered illegal. Google, like most review sites, does not allow the use of money, discounts, gifts, or other rewards for reviews.

<u>**(F) Ask for referrals:**</u> Using the testimonial form you created, add this question: "do you know of anyone who may be in need of my services?" Then ask for the phone numbers or email addresses of the people they are referring. Offer a "refer a friend" program: Give your customers an incentive for successfully referring a friend or family member. A free gift or gift certificate is a great way to thank your customers. Some companies send something as simple as a $5 Starbucks gift card – and the customers really appreciate it. You can always offer a $25 gift card if a referral turns into a customer. Referrals are easier to get if you are offering services like auto repair or house cleaning but everyone will eventually need the services of an electrician.

<u>**(G) This may be redundant...**</u> since I have already mentioned the "Customer Service Feedback Form" but ask your customers how you are doing in a digital format. You can use sites like surveymonkey.com to do this or you can create your own and send it via mail or email. Are they pleased with your electrical products or services? What can you do to make their experience better? What are their current needs or concerns?

When you receive your feedback – take it all in and see where you can implement changes in your business. Ask the customer to contact you before they leave negative comments online. This will give you an opportunity to correct any problems. *Strive to receive positive comments* but don't take any negative comments personal either! Make sure you thank your customer who took the time to fill it out. When you finally do implement changes – let them know. They will love to hear that their voices were heard.

(H) Connect with your customers on social media: Follow and interact with your customers on a few social media platforms. If you see them promoting their own business, help them share it as well. This will help increase the chances that they will do the same for you in return. If they have a website and a blog – pop in and read one of their blogs every now and then and leave a comment (or bring it up the next time you speak to them; for example say "I loved your blog about your housecleaning techniques, your tips and pictures were very helpful!")

(I) Provide outstanding customer service: 70% of the buying experience is based on how the customer feels they are being treated. Make sure your customers are receiving great customer service and listen to their needs. Act on the results of every Customer Service Feedback Form. Strive to get better and let your customer know that you took their advice.

(J) Reach out to your customers regularly: Give your customer a phone call or send them a card. Check in on them and see how they are doing. They may end up informing you that they have been meaning to reach out to you for electrical service work or something to that effect. Even if they do not, they will still be very thankful that you checked in on them. Customers don't forget these things!

> *"The only way to serve your company's interest is to serve your customer's interest."* - **Philip Kotler**

(K) Give your customer a thank you gift: Along the same lines as the "refer a friend" program, let your customers know you are grateful they chose YOUR electrical service company over the many others. Send them a handwritten note with a small gift, % off next purchase, gift card, etc. In today's social media world, customers will love it and may even give you a shout-out with a picture of the service that you performed (fixed a switch, fan, etc.,) on social media (giving you free marketing in return).

(L) Remind your customers about services you provide: Sometimes customers don't know you provide additional services and may end up unintentionally going with someone else. Remind them every so often of the services you provide. For example, maybe you were hired to add a receptacle to the garage and noticed that they had an electric vehicle. You could tell them about how your company offers EV Level 1 charger upgrades to EV Level 2 for a faster charge. The customer may had classified you as a simple electrician not knowing that you are keeping up with modern technology. Who knows, they may have been searching for someone to upgrade their electric vehicles charging capabilities and you may have lost that business. You can do this many different ways like in your newsletters, stories and pictures on social media, an email or card every couple months or so, etc.

(M) Exceed Expectations: most companies don't even meet customer's expectations, let alone exceed them. Find a way to stand out! Can you offer a free upgrade on a service? Can you perform a free service, such as changing out a light bulb for an elderly customer? Customers love receiving a random surprise or freebies that are completely unexpected.

(N) Become a problem solver and a helper: This can be challenging at times, especially if you have an angry customer. Make it a goal to turn that "anger" around to make them feel that you did everything in your power to fix and address their problem. If you can, go out of your way to help the angry customer, you may end up turning them into "lifetime" customer. Don't ignore complaints and correct as quickly as possible. I have seen small electrical companies go out of their way to make a customer happy even when the actual fault was a larger utility company's disturbing behavior. Larger companies tend to be more abusive to customer concerns so sometimes it is up to the smaller electrical service providers to take the high road. Believe me, this pays off in dividends in the future. Just put yourself in the customer's shoes.

(O) Drive clean vehicles and make sure to have a clean appearance. Have a "branded" look among all your employees. If someone saw your employee standing in line at a convenience store, would they know that they worked for your electrical business? If you offer vehicles to employees, ask them to wash the company vehicle once a month or more. It is the least that an employee can do since you are paying for gas and lessening the wear and tear on the employee's own personal vehicle. Have a clean appearance when you arrive at the residence or business that you are servicing. If your shoes are dirty, keep disposable shoe covers (booties) on all your vehicles. They're inexpensive and leave a lasting impression with the customer. One last thing, clean up after your work is done. There is nothing more disrespectful than driving off and leaving a mess for a customer to have to clean up.

7) Retargeting

Do you ever get that feeling that big brother is watching? Well you have a good reason for that feeling. Retargeting marketing allows you to target specific visitors to your website, social media page, etc., with specific ads with the long-term intent of convincing them to purchase your products or services. Retargeting can be simply triggered by an individual doing a search for a particular product or service, in our case, electrical services. Have you ever shopped for an item on the internet only to be bombarded with advertisements for that same item even when you are just casually "surfing the web"? Retargeting usually has a higher conversion rate because this marketing method shows "ads" to the visitors that have already visited your pages or searched for your products or services.

A conversion occurs when a visitor to your website, social media pages, etc., completes a desired goal, such as filling out a form or making a purchase.

To set up a retargeting campaign, go to ads.google.com and get started in three easy steps. 1) Create your campaign, 2) Select where you want to advertise(certain interest and demographics), 3) Set your budget. Now when people click on your website, you can basically "follow" them around and remind them about your business and services.

8) Press Release (PR Release)

Usually when you think of a press release, you have images in your head of a newspaper with a big header screaming out the big "headlines" of the day. Even if you have a website and are familiar with SEO, there's still a big chance you haven't used a press release before. I'm sure you've heard about the notion of press re-

leases but have you heard the benefits of SEO as it relates to press releases? **Is it worth spending your time dealing with a press release?** The short answer is <u>yes</u>. Press releases are still relevant and probably will be for a long time to come, not only for search engine optimization, but for marketing, in general.

"Is it worth spending your time dealing with a press release?"

The short answer - yes!

By writing a good press release and having it distributed to some of the top sites on the web, you get to lead the conversation and you get to have it with more people. You set the narrative... What do you want people to think about when they hear your name or your business name? Today, more than ever, people like to see or read the most current, most relevant and the most up-to-date information about products, services and businesses. Everyone likes a success story and they truly want to see smaller companies like yours in the news. Getting in the news gives you credibility, social proof and heaps of embedded authority. It also makes

> **What Is A Press Release?**
> *A press release is a short, official statement sent to the media for publicity that can immediatly:*
> *1) Get You Featured on High-Traffic Sites*
> *2) Demonstrate Social Proof*
> *3) Improve Your SEO & Build Backlinks*
> *4) Develop Your Brand Awareness*
> *5) Improve Your Online Reputation*

2 NEWS

PRESS RELEASE

Ozburn Electric Enhances Their Metro Atlanta Outdoor Lighting Division.

Residential, Commercial, Retail and Industrial Security Light: The First Security Provider That You Should Consider. Ozburn Electric of Covington, GA, in conjunction with it's outdoor lighting division, has made it a...

Saturday, February 8th 2020, 12:00 AM PST

POPULAR STORIES

Lake Tahoe's Fluctuating Clarity Worsens Amid Wet Winter
August 1st, 11:27 AM PDT

Sierra Front: Three Fires Burning Near Hallelujah Junction
14 hrs 49 mins ago

NHP: Investigating Fatal Crash On Pyramid Highway
August 1st, 11:58 PM PDT

Nevada Passes Bill to Mail All Voters Ballots Amid Pandemic
18 hrs 25 mins ago

SPCA Begins Accepting Donations for New Thrift Store
5 hrs 19 mins ago

Residential, Commercial, Retail and Industrial Security Light: The First Security Provider That You Should Consider.

Ozburn Electric of Covington, GA, in conjunction with it's outdoor lighting division, has made it a goal to create a safer experience for residential properties, commercial

81

you far more visible and the best thing is you get to set the narrative and tell the story that you want to tell.

Press releases can also be seen as a "citation" or direct link to your website. You can add links and other crucial information to a press release. The press releases that Power Surge SEO offer can distribute your company information to some of the heavy hitters in news and media like USA Today, The New York Times, The Wall Street Journal, Bloomberg Business Week, and more. The point is really not to make it to the "big time" but rather to get your name and links out to the masses. A press release is an excellent way to build authority through meta tags, backlinks, links, and more.

The Press releases that we offer at Power Surge SEO are delivered to over 1,400 syndicated outlets such as Bloomberg, USA Today, The New York Times, and many more. A well-written press release is perfect, not only for exclaiming the virtues of your business, but also for giving your website excellent citations for Google's algorithm to rely on when someone is performing a search for your products and services.

9) Webinars & Podcasts

By introducing webinars and podcasts, you can possibly become what some refer to as an "influencer". Webinars give you the chance to demonstrate and showcase your brand and electrical knowledge to a targeted, live audience. You can also engage them, gather feedback and answer all their questions on the spot. Just imagine a Zoom meeting where you are the host and you get to share your knowledge with either customers or people that you have invited to the meeting. You can then "syndicate" where you others may pickup your webinar and share with their audience. You can invite peers or electrical wholesalers in your industry to participate or even invite industry product manufacturers to interview. You can then take the audio from the webinar and produce a Podcast from it. Your podcast show can be hosted by sites like Podbean, Libsyn, iTunes, etc.

-With your own podcast, you get to become the industry expert.-

82

10) PPL (Pay-Per-Lead)

Pay-Per-Lead is where you don't actually pay until a valid customer lead is delivered to your company. This type of marketing is usually done by qualified agencies that specialize in PPL. Pay-Per-Lead is a marketing service in which the clients (you and your electrical business) of a PPL marketing agency only pay for leads that express interest in electrical services. Early on, you and the PPL agency come to an agreement about how much each lead will cost and how many they should deliver each month. Leads are defined as conversion events such as signing up to receive emails, placing a call, or using your website's contact form. Your agreement with your PPL marketing agency will determine how many leads you should expect each month, which simplifies your marketing budget.

Pay-Per-Lead (PPL) agencies only get paid once they deliver interested visitors who are ready to take the next step with your services. This means they have a much greater incentive to bring leads to your business.

Some examples of Pay-Per-Lead are Angie's List, Home Advisor, Yelp, and more. A typical fee from one of these agencies range from around $7 to $20 per lead. One caveat, these agencies like to offer a customer lead to a few different electricians. For example, if a potential customer (lead) uses Home Advisor to list a residential project, Home Advisor, in turn, will give the potential customer's contact information to several "vetted" electricians for a "fee". It is up to you to then secure the lead. Sometimes securing the lead can be as simple as being the first to respond but sometimes it does come down to price. Just to warn you, it is a lot easier for a "vetted" one-truck electrician with no overhead to offer a lower price than a vetted ten-truck electrical company with a lot of overhead. That being said, PPL is still a viable option but not for everyone. If you decide to participate in PPL, one thing that it does provide is a great external link to your website since these agencies typically have your contact information posted on their website.

Notes

11) EDDM™ - Every Door Direct Mailer™ - USPS™

The United States Postal Service (USPS™) offers a paid service called "Every Door Direct Mail™" (EDDM™). This service is to promote your small business in your local community. As an electrical contractor, it may benefit you to target specific zip codes with your products and services. The EDDM™ program can help you send postcards, coupons, and flyers to the right customers. I will show you how you can use the EDDM™ Online Tool to map ZIP Code and neighborhoods—even filter by age, income, or household size using U.S. Census data. The really nice thing about EDDM™ is the fact that if you do offer residential electrical services, you can pinpoint specific zip codes based on the family's annual income.
Here is a synopsis of how you can mail out direct mailers such as postcards to potential customers.

1) First, you have to open up an account with the United States Postal Service at https://www.usps.com. This is simple and free and chances are you already have an account with the postal service.

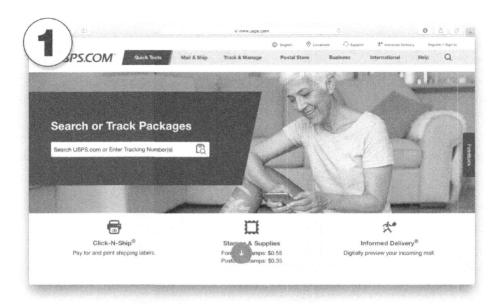

2) Second, once you have opened up an account, select the "Business" tab at the top. This will open up a selection of options for you to pick from. You will then want to go down to the left and click on the option "Every Door Direct Mail™".

3) Third, you are now in a window where you can enter your target zip code (the zip code that you want to target for your customer base). *Word of caution here*, you will need to pick a zip code that is within driving range for your company unless you want to incur shipping charges. You will have to deliver or ship your direct mailers to the post office in the zip code that you choose. USPS will not come to your office and get these mailers. One of the reasons that you get such a fair price for this service is because you have to basically do all of the work. In the long run, it saves you a lot of money that can be used in other areas of your marketing budget.

One of the reasons that you get such a fair price for this service is because you have to basically do all of the work. In the long run, it saves you a lot of money that can be used in other areas of your marketing budget.

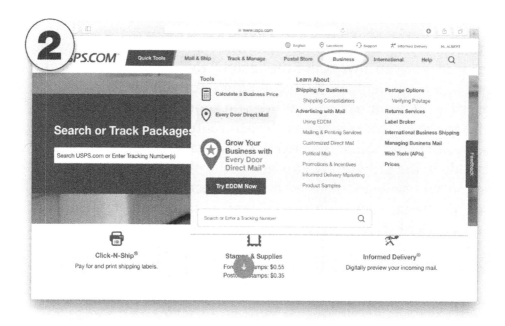

Zoomed
In view

3) *continued*

In this same window, if you don't know the zip code but you know the area well, you can always use the "zoom" tool that is located at the bottom left of the map. Keep zooming until you visually find the area that you want to target. When you zoom up high enough, you will see the zip codes along with each route in the zip code. Once you see the zip code of the area that you want to target, enter that zip code in the browser bar just above the map. By entering the zip code, it will now populate with the correct routes inside this zip code. If you have any problems, please contact the EDDM Support team as seen below.

Contact The EDDM Support Team

If you have specific questions about EDDM mailings, contact the EDDM Retail Service customer support team (USPS National Customer Support Center) at 1-877-747-6249.

4) After placing the chosen zip code in the browser bar above the map, you will then be able to see your zip code enlarged showing every route (gray) inside your zip code. It is important to note that there may be a few routes or many routes inside your zip code. It is all based on the population of that zip code. Once you are in this window, you will be able to take your prompt tool arrow (your mouse) and hover over each and every route inside the zip code. As you hover over each route, the route will turn a pinkish-purple. If you select a route, you get to see all the demographics of that route above the map but below the zip code.

> *"Low paid salesmen are expensive. High paid salesmen are cheap."*
> - Philip Kotler

Call us today at
1-888-235-4SEO (4736)
www.PowerSurgeSEO.com

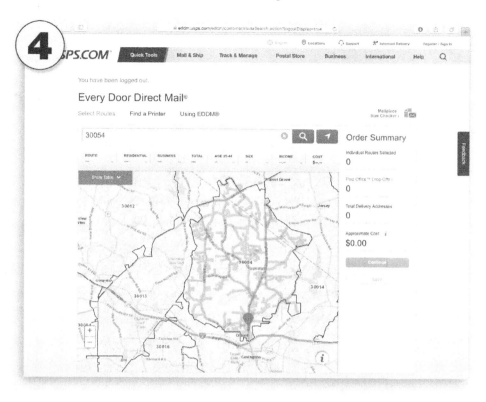

Notes

5) Once you have selected a zip code and a route, all the information pertaining to that zip code and route will be shown above the map and below the browser bar.

  A) Zip code in the browser bar

  B) Highlighted Route of the zip code

  C) Demographics for that route inside that zip code.

  D) Order Summary -

This shows what you have selected including the route inside the zip code, the number of Post Office locations that service this route, the total number of addresses that your mailer will deliver to and the costs to deliver the total amount.

1	2	3	4	5	6	7	8
ROUTE	RESIDENTIAL	BUSINESS	TOTAL	AGE 25-44	SIZE	INCOME	COST
30054-R086 ⌄	503 ⌄	0 ⌄	503	23% ⌄	2.85 PPL ⌄	$90.40K ⌄	$96.07

1) Route = 30054-R-086

This is Zip Code 30054, Route 086. There can be many routes in a zip code. There is always at least one route in a zip code.

2) Residential population = 503

This represents the residential population inside this zip code and this route (30054-R-086). This number will change with every zip and route entered.

3) Business population = 0

This represents the amount of businesses inside this zip code and route. In this case, there are zero businesses located in this zip code and this route.

4) Total population = 503

This represents the population inside this zip code and route. there happens to be 503 persons living at this zip code and route.

5) Age 25-44 Demographics = 23% make up of this route's population. You can "toggle" and select the age group of your preference. If you want to target 34 years old individuals, you can target 34 years old individuals only. It's up to you. This example shows that this zip code and route is made up of 23% of the age group of 25-44 years of age.

6) Size = 2.85 people per household
The average household size of each route. This zip code and route averages 2.85 people per household.

91

7) Income = $90,400
The average household income of each route.

8) Cost = $96.07 (to mail a postcard to each of 503 addresses in this route)
 This is a great deal since you can touch 503 households with a direct mailer that showcases your services.

6) Once you have selected your zip code and route, you are now ready to drop off at (or ship to) the Post Office in order for them to deliver your mailers. You will need to physically take your mailing to the Post Office locations that will deliver to your selected EDDM routes. You can choose to ship your mailers to those Post Office locations but it can be expensive and it is always nice to be there, in person, just in case you have done something wrong (remember, we are talking about the government!). If you deliver and there is a problem, you can then correct your error, immediately at the Post Office, or take them back to the office and correct your mistake. You can then drive back to the Post Office with the corrected mailers. If you ship to a Post Office, you have to make sure that you have done everything correctly or the USPS will not correct your error. Don't forget that the USPS is ran by the government and you are getting a discount to do this job yourself and do it correctly.

For more information, contact your EDDM support team!
If you have specific questions about EDDM mailings, contact the EDDM Retail Service customer support team (USPS National Customer Support Center) at 1-877-747-6249.

By utilizing the EDDM™ service offered by the USPS, you get have several choices from the demographics dashboard to send custom direct mail to the zip code of your choice. **Please study the website carefully.**

https://www.usps.com/business/every-door-direct-mail.htm

Here are a few more things that you need to know about EDDM™. (as of Oct. 2020)

> Call us today at
> 1-888-235-4SEO(4736)
> www.PowerSurgeSEO.com

<u>You Need To Design & Print Your Mailpiece</u> (Hint: We Can Help!) Follow direct mail design best practices to create effective EDDM advertising pieces. Sending actionable mail with a clear offer and call to action will help generate customer responses.

• You must send a direct mailer to everyone in the chosen route of the chosen zip code. You cannot "cherry pick". The minimum mail piece size is 3.5 inches high, 5 inches long, and 0.007 inch thick, but to be considered a flat, a piece must exceed at least one of the minimum dimensions noted in the accompanying illustration — without a permit and without the expense of list purchasing. The mailer must provide enough mail pieces to cover either every active residential or every active residential and business combined delivery on one or more carrier routes serviced by the retail office (up to a maximum of 5,000 pieces per mailing).

• Acceptance at all USPS retail locations.

• Only Standard Mail flats accepted (see diagram below).

• Mailing destined for the local delivery area.

• Per-piece weight limit of 3.3 oz.

• Maximum of 5,000 mail pieces, per mailer, per day, per unit.

- No permit is required; a new universal indicia can be used for EDDM-Retail.

- No trust account payment accepted.

- Other rules and regulations may apply. Check your local Post Office for more information.

I only touched briefly on the United States Postal Service's EDDM™. There is more to this highly affordable service and it requires a little "hands-on" approach. You will have to get the post cards or direct mail designed, printed (local or online printer) and then delivered to your location. Once you set up the zip codes and routes, you will then have to sort, bundle and tag all of the mail, usually in bundles or 50's or 100's. After tagging the direct mail or postcards, you will then have to deliver to the post office within

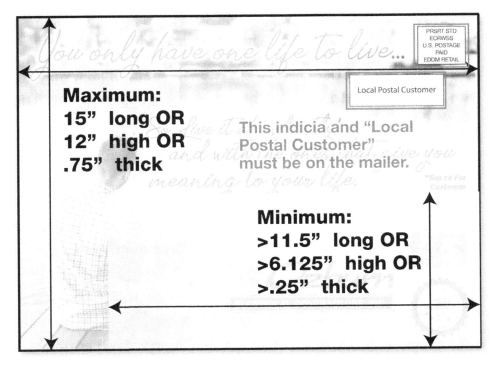

A good standard size is 9" wide x 6.5" high.

the zip code of where you want the media mailed. It sounds difficult but it is a lot easier than it sounds. For more information about this great program, contact your local post office or go to www.usps.com/everydoordirectmail.

12) Programs (Gift Cards, Giveaways, Contest, etc.,)

At the top of the Marketing Pyramid are programs such as gift cards, discounts, giveaways, contests, and more. Programs like these are an excellent way to build your brand relatively inexpensively. This marketing technique has been around for years and even prior to the advent of the internet. Businesses have been using giveaways and sweepstakes, for as long as marketing has existed, hoping to generate interest and sales for their products or services.

These days, you can use social media to drive a program such as a contest or a giveaway. Not only do you create a loyal following, people win prizes and nobody is any happier than a prize winner. Don't hold social media contests and give away products and prizes just because you see other companies doing it. There are a lot of sound, proven reasons that social media contests have been proven to work. *One Caveat.* Please follow all social media rules and regulations! You would not want to get in trouble with the big boys! (Facebook, Google, etc.,)

These rules and regulations may change often so make sure to check often and completely abide by the rules. For instance, if you are running a contest or giveaway on Facebook, please go to Facebook's Rules and Regulations page or to the following address to read more about their latest guidelines.

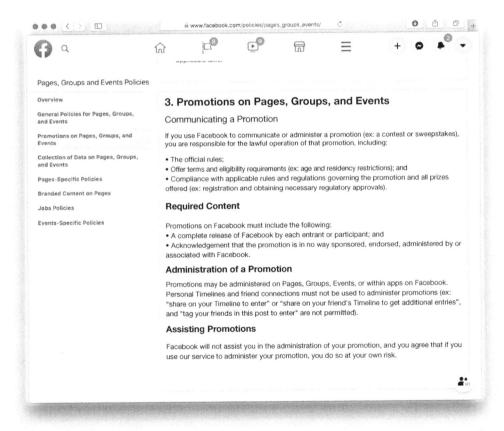

https://www.facebook.com/policies/pages_groups_events/

Gift cards are probably the easiest ways to put a smile on a face and gain instant loyalty. Gift cards can be used not only as a prizes for contests, they can also be used to diffuse an issue or to show thanks for customer loyalty. Giveaways can be comprised of gift cards or any prize that you want to give away that follows local jurisdiction's laws and social media rules and regulations. I have seen my electrical clients give away prizes that consist of gift cards, lapel pins, electrical services, discounts for electrical services, televisions, and more! Every winner was thrilled. Even the ones that just got a simple lapel pin left happy.

Another type of giveaway that wins over the local community and gains customer loyalty is to sponsor events and contest in the community in conjunction with other vendors, hospitals, nursing homes, chamber of commerce, Lion's Club, YMCA, civic organizations, retirement centers and more. LED TVs are exceptionally inexpensive these days and you can get a lot of press for less than $200. Give an inexpensive LED TV to a nursing home, hospital, school PTA, etc., as a raffle gift and make sure that the local paper, radio or television media know about the event. This $200 event will gain you about $1,000 in press coverage and probably increase your company's brand in the community.

Also as part of your "Programs" marketing, make sure to become more active in the community and possibly join one or more civic organizations. Most service organizations are made up of people, like you, who are business owners, who have varying areas of interests and want to help the local community while networking with each other. You are not limited to these particular organizations. There are plenty out in your community under these or other names.

- Chamber of Commerce
- Lion's Club
- Check your community for more!
- Kiwanis Club
- Optimist Club
- Rotary Club
- The Shriner's

Most service organizations are made up of people, like you, who are business owners, who have varying areas of interests and want to help the local community while networking with each other.

Notes

_____

_____

_____

_____

_____

_____

_____

_____

_____

_____

_____

_____

_____

_____

_____

_____

_____

_____

_____

_____

_____

_____

_____

_____

_____

_____

_____

_____

_____

_____

_____

_____

_____

_____

"Today you have to run faster to stay in the same place."
                                            - Philip Kotler

Did You Know?...

In 2020, there are over 625,000 active electricians employed in the United States and the numbers are expected to grow by almost 15% by 2024. The demand for tradeworkers is growing exponitially and there will be over 715,000 electricians in the next four years. This may seem like a lot of new electricians but the demand for tradeworks, such as electricians, far surpasses the supply.

Here are some more lesser known facts about electricians.

• Master electricians train almost as long as doctors.

• In most cases, electricians have to pass a "color blind" test. This is because color is used to determine wire gauges and more. It could actually be dangerous to be color blind in the electrical trade.

• There have been many famous celebrities that have started out as electricians (you may be the next one!)
- *Elvis Presley* worked for Crown Electrical in the '50s.
- *George Harrison* of the **Beatles** started out as an Electrician's Apprentice.
- *Rowan Atkinson*, now famous for being Mr Bean, has a Masters degree in Electrical Engineering.

Here are a few others who worked in the electrical field.

Liam Cunningham - "Davos" in the *Game of Thrones*
Albert Einstein - Worked for his father's electrical company
Alfred Hitchcock - Famous director, producer and screenwriter

Notes

Did you know that the state of New York leads the nation with the highest average electricial pay at $63,328 per year. South Dakota is at the bottom of the scale with an average of $35,906 per electrician. Alaska is measured as the best state for jobs for Electricians, and Hawaii is the worst.
Source - www.Zippia.com

Your Marketing Strategy

Creating a Marketing Strategy

I touched on what a marketing plan or strategy is in the first few pages of this book. Overall, a marketing plan or strategy refers to a business's overall game plan for reaching prospective consumers (leads) and turning (converting) them into customers of the products or services that a business provides.

In the last 100 pages, I have given you plenty of information to start with. Now that you are familiar with the basics of the marketing pyramid and more, it's time to implement a marketing strategy for your business.

67,000 searches are performed on Google every second

93% of all online experiences begin with a search engine

80% of users <u>IGNORE</u> paid ads in search results

58% of searches come from **MOBILE**

46% of all Google searches are **LOCAL**   SOURCE: SEOTribunal.com

---

In the second half of this book, We will answer some questions that will show you how you can create an action plan for your own electrical services business.

First of all, it's important to recognize there are three keys to success with your website and eventually your business:

• **Company Visibility!** We need to make sure that your website is fully optimized to show up in your organic listing when someone types in the key words that are important to you and your business. Remember, the goal with SEO is whenever someone types an electrical "key word" into the search engine (Google, Yahoo, Bing, etc.,), your business shows up on the first page. This is impossible unless you have the right plan and right people involved that can make this work for you. Remember that our goal is to get you on Google page 1. Google has now rolled out "Google My Business" (GMB) which we will touch on later in this book.

• **Conversion** - As you recall, a conversion occurs when a visitor to your website completes a desired goal, such as filling out a form or making a purchase. This is our ultimate goal for your website. We want a visitor to be "called to action" and become a convert to your products and services.

• Make sure that your website is **"Mobile Friendly"**.

According to a CNBC article, by the year 2025, 75% of the world will only use their smartphones to access the internet.

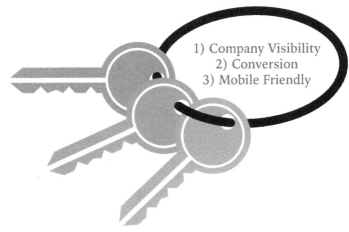

1) Company Visibility
2) Conversion
3) Mobile Friendly

Notes

_____
_____
_____
_____
_____
_____
_____
_____
_____
_____
_____
_____

Key Strategies That You Need To Incorporate Now.

The following are some of the strategies we used with our clients here at PowerSurgeSEO.com. These strategies, if incorporated correctly, will definitely increase your chances of success as an electrical entrepreneur.

After reading this book about the marketing strategies needed to be performed in your business marketing plan, if you still don't feel comfortable about DIY, then please consult a professional marketing agency that specializes in more than just building a website.

Feel free to contact PowerSurgeSEO.com as well. Simply send an email to help@powersurgeseo.com (or call us at 1-888-235-4SEO(4736)) and we will try our best to answer your questions.

Now I will discuss how our agency would start working with a client. Let's imagine that you are Terry Ozburn (our example client) and your electrical services company is Ozburn Electrical Contractors, Inc.

Using this as a starting point, let's create your marketing plan. Let's start with the "Customer Onboarding".

"Welcome aboard Mr. Ozburn and Ozburn Electrical Contractors, Inc.. It's great to have you aboard! Let's start by filling out the following 'Electrician's Online Marketing Checklist' sheet."

"Mr. Ozburn, the reason that we want you to fill out this sheet is that it will give us a benchmark of where to start when it comes to servicing your marketing needs."

Second, we make sure that your website is designed and developed to be fully optimize for SEO purposes. In most cases we have to completely rebuild clients websites because, like some electrical jobs, it is easier to start over and do it correctly rather than waste time trying to recover a site to the point of it being useful.

We also need to make sure that the site is mobile friendly. As stated earlier, it is vital that your website is mobile friendly because the majority of customers will be viewing your site on their smart devices.

Pages 105-108 will ask you the questions that we ask our new customers from our "Electrician's Online Marketing Checklist". Try to "mentally" answer them to the best of your ability. If it helps, write your answers out on a blank piece of paper. *Let's Go!*

Electrician's Online Marketing Checklist

Question 1 - *Answer on p. 109*

1) Is your website properly optimized for search (SEO)?

Question 2 - *Answer on p. 114*

2) Do you have your main keyword in the Site Title and Tagline and H1 Tags on each of the pages of your website? (E.G. Your City Electrician | Your Company Name)

Question 3 - *Answer on p. 117*

3) Do you have individual pages for each of your core services?

Question 4 - *Answer on p. 119*

4) Do you have individual pages for the brands that you service?

Question 5 - *Answer on p. 120*

5) Do you have unique content on each of the pages of your website?

Question 6 - *Answer on p. 123*

6) Are you helping Google understand your true service area?

Question 7 - *Answer on p. 134*

7) Have you claimed your Google My Business (GMP) page?

Question 8 - *Answer on p. 137*

8) Does your website rank on page one for your most important keywords like "your city electrician", "your city electrical"?

Question 9 - *Answer on p. 140*

9) Is your website optimized for conversion?
(turning visitors in to callers)

Question 10 - *Answer on p. 140*

10) Do you have the Phone Number in the top right corner on every page?

Question 11 - *Answer on p. 141*

11) Are you using authentic images/video? Photo of the owner, photo of your trucks, photo of your team, etc?

Question 12 - *Answer on p. 149*

12) Do you have a compelling Call To Action after ever blog of text?

Question 13 - *Answer on p. 156*

13) Is your website MOBILE site friendly?

Question 14 - Answer on p. 157

14) Are you consistently creating new content, blogging and creating new inbound links back to your website?

Question 15 - Answer on p. 165

15) Do you understand the importance of NAP...name, address, and phone number?

Question 16 - Answer on p. 170

16) Do you know the Login Username and Passwords for every website or service used by your business?

Question 17 - Answer on p. 171

17) Does your address(s) represent an actual office space, a virtual office or shared space within an office used by other businesses?

Question 18 - Answer on p. 172

18) Is your business located in your home? If so, do you use your home's physical address for your business's physical address? Do you have a Post Office Box number?

Question 19 - Answer on p. 174

19) Have any of your listed locations moved in the past 10 years? If so, please list any known former addresses or phone numbers.

Question 20 - Answer on p. 175

20) Are any other phone numbers, whether call tracking, toll free, local, or vanity being used to represent your business locations or any other type business at your location? Please list and explain.

Question 21 - Answer on p. 177

21) How long has the website existed at this domain, and have there been previous domain names in the past 10 years?

Question 22 - Answer on p. 181

22) Please list out all of the major services and/or products that your company offers.

Question 23 - Answer on p. 183

23) Are you active, in any way, on social media? Personal or Business?

Question 24 - Answer on p. 184

24) Are you leveraging email marketing? (MailChimp, Aweber, Constant Contact, etc.,)

Question 25 - Answer on p. 186

25) Are you sending out monthly newsletters either print or email?

Question 26 - Answer on p. 187

26) Are you taking advantage of Pay-Per-Click (PPC) or Pay-Per-Lead (PPL) or any other type paid online advertising?

Question 27 - Answer on p. 196

27) Are you using a CRM (Customer Relationship Management) software such as ServiceTitan or Housecall Pro?

Question 28 - Answer on p. 198

28) Are you using Google Search Control (GSC)? *(fomerly known as Google Webmaster Tools, and Google Webmaster Central)*?

Question 29 - Answer on p. 202

29) Do you have any idea how much money you are spending (ROI) on marketing your Business? Monthly?, Annually?

Question 30 - Answer on p. 213

30) Do you feel overwhelmed just at the thought of doing your own marketing?

Now we will answer the questions by using www.OzburnElectrical.com as our benchmark. Answering these questions will give you a roadmap in devising a marketing strategy for your electrical business. As we answer these questions, you will see how important it is to have a sound marketing plan to showcase your electrical services company's products and services.

Many of the forms seen in this book can be found at: www.PowerSurgeSEO.com/Forms.

Now that the **"Electrician's Online Marketing Checklist"** sheet is filled out, please follow along as we examine the answers that Mr. Ozburn gave us. It is important to see how to you can incorporate some of these strategies into your electrical company's marketing plan. Just imagine your business in place of Mr. Ozburn's electrical services company.

It may be helpful to go to the Ozburn Electrical Contractors, Inc. website at, www.OzburnElectrical.com, and use it as a baseline to follow along answering these questions.

Question 1

Is your website properly optimized for search (SEO)?

In the situation with Mr. Ozburn's website, the answer was "no". His mediocre website was created by a huge company (that was spun off from a phone book company). They put little effort into on-page and off-page SEO and were charging Mr. Ozburn a substantial amount of money each month. It seems that their true intentions were to make the bulk of their profits by charging additionally for PPC and PPL. When my company looked at the site, we determined that we really needed to rebuild it and make it fully optimized for SEO.

We rebuilt the site that you see at www.OzburnElectrical.com but it did not stop there. We got very busy with link building and citation development so the site could start to develop authority in the electrical industry.

Place Internal Links in Your Content.

When we started building out each individual page for www.OzburnElectrical.com, we used many internal links. Internal links are links in your content that are connected to other pages or articles within your website. Search engine crawlers use links to transfer from one page to another and to discover new web pages.

Like a spider building a web, we linked each page internally via select keywords in the content of each page. These links were made possible by the easy word linking features in WordPress. All you have to do is, as you build each page and add content, select and highlight keywords in the content and then link (copy and paste) to the URL of other internal pages on your website. Using internal links is like marking a trail for website visitors to explore, therefore creating higher traffic on your site.

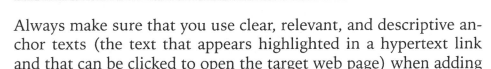

Linking pictures, internal web pages, external websites and more is easy by clicking on this button in WordPress. Also see p. 159.

Always make sure that you use clear, relevant, and descriptive anchor texts (the text that appears highlighted in a hypertext link and that can be clicked to open the target web page) when adding

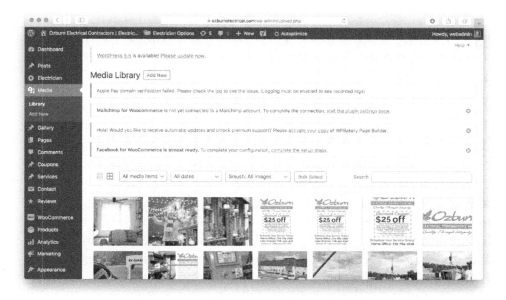

internal links on your page. This will help the reader get a clear grasp of what that link is all about and how it relates to your page.

Provide External or Outbound Links.
You may notice that we put a lot of emphasis on "links". It doesn't end with internal links inside the website. We than started creating external links. External links are similar to internal but rather than linking to other pages on your website, these link to pages found across the internet. External page links also helps crawlers further understand your content. If you practice linking to websites that are related to your topic that have high domain authority (DA), you increase the credibility of your page, which is important for overall SEO. Both internal links and external links are an important part of the SEO process.

Spread secondary/LSI keywords in Your Content.
As you write content for your website, make sure to use words associated with your products or services. These word are known as LSI keywords or Latent Semantic Indexing (LSI). In the case of an electrician's website, you may write content that includes keywords such as "Atlanta Electrician" or "Commercial Electrician located in Trenton, NJ". LSI keywords can be peppered among the content as "wiring", "wing nuts", "wire nuts", "can lights", "ceil-

ing fan", etc. When Google's algorithm sees this information, it helps to determine that your site, is indeed, a functioning electrician's website.

Do the Necessary Image Optimization on Your Website.

Using good resolution images in your content will make the information you present easier to understand and makes your page interesting. Images also contribute to your page's overall ranking as it relates to SEO and SERPs. Try to have your workers or yourself take nice, clean pictures (with their smartphones) before the job, during the job, and after the job. This way you will always have documentation for the job, but also great high resolution photos that you can use on your website. When uploading your photos to your website (or Google My Business, etc.), ideally you want to add a keyword in your image file name, title, and alt text. As seen in the this picture, you have the opportunity to enter information for the Alternative Text, the Title, the Caption, and the Description. <u>Make sure to enter this information in for good on-page SEO.</u>

Your images are located in the "Media Library" of your WordPress website. You can also add this information as you build your site and upload your images. Just don't leave them blank because this is vital for good on-page SEO.

Use high-quality images and do not forget to size them to their intended display (for faster page load time) before uploading it on your site. Remember, our goal is to have a home page load-up of around 3

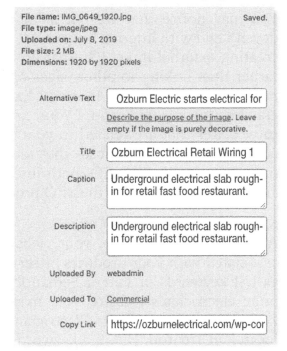

to 4 seconds. The more that you do up front the less the hosting server has to think about it.

When creating the new site, we created pages for every option of service that Ozburn Electric offered to it's customers. When we created those pages, we made sure to write content specific to those pages. We also made sure to use the internal and external links. We put in a Coupon page, locations served page, Residential services page, Commercial services page, Industrial services page, and much more. Some would think that it is overkill but we see it as fully optimizing the website for great SEO. Our intentions are to have a page for every Google electrical search query out there. If a customer searches for "Automation and Controls", we have a page built for it. If a customer searches for "Electric Vehicle Charger Installation", we have a page for it. After we finish our jobs, we ended up with over 100 pages of fully "on-page" optimized and customized pages for Ozburn Electrical Contractors, Inc., Each page had it's own unique title and H1 tag stating something using

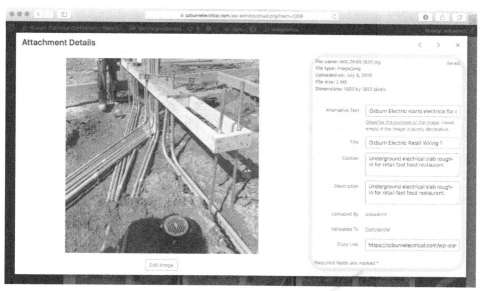

Image optimization by adding the correct Alternative Text, Title, Caption, and Description. These images are located in the media library of your WordPress website.

keywords found on the page. We had images with alt tags containing keywords. Even our urls contained page keywords.

After completion, we then submitted a full SML sitemap to Google Search Console and Bing Webmaster. Google and the other search engines then sent out their robots or "bots" to crawl and index the page. All this works together to make the www.OzburnElectrical.com site a great site for excellent SERP results for those searching for an electrician.

Question 2

Do you have your main keyword in the Site Title and Tagline and H1 Tags on each of the pages of your website?
(E.G. Your City Electrician | Your Company Name)

Use Concise Page Titles & Page H1 Tags
Once again, Mr. Ozburn's site did not have a correct Site Title tag. While building his new website out, we included an SEO friendly Site Title and Tagline. This can be changed inside the admin section of your website under the "Settings" (General Settings) tab. The titles are one of the most important factors for optimized SEO. Web crawlers will use be used by the search engines to check your title tags and each page's H1 header tags for search queries. Make your page H1 titles unique and eye-catching. The title should also be de-

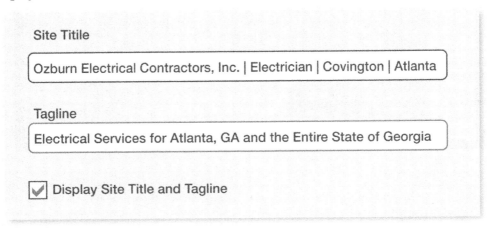

Site Title

Ozburn Electrical Contractors, Inc. | Electrician | Covington | Atlanta

Tagline

Electrical Services for Atlanta, GA and the Entire State of Georgia

☑ Display Site Title and Tagline

Heading Tags For SEO

\<h1\> Most Important

\<h2\> Second Most Important

\<h3\> Third Most Important

\<h4\> Fourth Most Important

\<h5\> Fifth Most Important

\<h6\> Sixth Most Important

scriptive, concise, and should encapsulate what your page is all about.

As you see here in the Site Title, we have the full company name, the world "Electrician" and then the service areas. It is important to put this information here for the search engine web crawlers to see and crawl.

When it comes to providing strong SEO web content, you must also have H1 header titles for each individual pages. You are probably wondering what "H1" means. The H1 is an HTML tag that indicates a heading on a website. An HTML tag is a snippet of code that tells your web browser how to display the content.

When it comes to your pages on the website, the "Headings" of each page can be comprised of six different heading tags — H1, H2, and so on. The H1 (very big and bold) is considered the most important tag, and the h6 (very tiny and probably not bold) is the least important. You want your H1 Header to be descriptive, concise, and should encapsulate what your page is all about. Here is an example of a H1 Header on Ozburn Electrical's home page.

You only have one location in WordPress to set your Site Title and Tag Line!

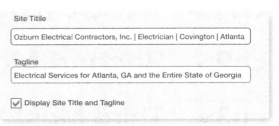

Make sure that each other page has a H1 Title Tag that includes the primary keyword you've set for the page. Do not forget to wrap your title in an H1 title tag — a piece of HTML code that tells search engines that the copy you wrapped is the page's title copy and an important element in your content. This can be easily done in the WordPress website page. You just simple type the headline that you want and then select the "H1" or "H2" selection to wrap your text.

H1 Tag (on Home Page) stating keywords for optimized SEO

116

Question 3

Do you have individual pages for each of your core services?

Once again, Mr. Ozburn's site did not have individual pages for each of the services that he offered. In total, his original website only had the standard few pages that you see on most sites; Home, About Us, Contact, and a Blog page.

While building his new site, we made sure to ask

INDUSTRIAL	COMMERCIAL	RESIDENTIAL

OUR ELECTRICAL SERVICES

OUR INDUSTRIAL BACKGROUND

24 HOUR SERVICE

SAFETY FIRST!

AIRFIELD LIGHTING CERTIFIED

COLOR INFRARED THERMOGRAPHY

CONTROL SYSTEMS INTEGRATION

CUSTOM CONTROL PANELS AND INSTALLATION

EV CHARGERS FOR INDUSTRIAL FACILITIES

ELECTROTECHNICAL PANEL BUILDER

the right questions to find out exactly what services that Ozburn Electrical offered to their customer base. We ended up with an astounding amount of pages (over 100 pages) that showcased each and every service that they offered in at least three different categories; Residential, Commercial, and Industrial.

Here are just a few of the *core services* that you may offer as an Electrical Contractor. Pick and choose the services that you provide and create individual website pages showcasing these services.

24 hour Service, 7 days a week
Airfield Lighting Certified
Color Infrared Thermography
Control Systems Integration
Custom Control Panels and Installation
EV Chargers for Industrial Facilities

Retail EV Charger Installation
Electrotechnical Panel Builder
Industrial Electrical Contractor
Industrial Electrical Engineering and Design
Industrial Electrical Inspector
Industrial Electrician
Industrial Emergency Power
Industrial Maintenance Electricians
Industrial Manufacturing and Production Facilities
Industrial Warehouse LED Lighting
LED Lighting Retro Fits
LEED Certified Electrician
Motion Controllers
Design/Build
Automation and Controls
Preventative Maintenance Programs
ConEst, Procore, Service Titan, Housecall Pro, etc.,
Commercial Electrical Contractor
Commercial Electrical Engineering and Design
Commercial Electrical Inspector
Commercial Electrician
Commercial Emergency Power
Commercial Maintenance Electricians
Commercial Manufacturing and Production Facilities
Commercial Warehouse LED Lighting
Outside Lineman
Parking Lot Lighting
PLC Programming and Automation
Powerhouse and Substation Technician
Preventative Maintenance
Robotics
Server Controllers
Variable Frequency Drives (VFD's)
Electrical Repairs
Panel Upgrades

Lighting Upgrades
Residential EV Charger Installation and upgrade
Surge Protection
Generator Installs and Repair
Ceiling Fan Installation
Outdoor and Motion Lighting
EV Charger installation (Level 1, Level 2, Fast DC Charger, etc.,)
Our Electricians are Certified and Trained (show Schooling)
Solar Power *and much more!*

When you are building out your website, it is critical to make a page for every service that you offer. By doing this, the Google-Bots, and BingBots, of the world, are able to crawl and index each and every page making it easier to suggest your website to any query that a potential customer is searching for. *This also helps in answering question 4.*

Question 4

Do you have individual pages for the brands that you service?

If you have specific brands that you service, such as product or manufacturer brands, you need to list them in individual pages also. For example, let's say that your automation and controls division only services Siemens' Automation and Controls products. You need to have a page that showcases your work with Siemens' Automation and Controls products. Tell the world, from one page, about how you are the best at programming Siemens' products. This is the same for all electrical brands including Klein Tools, Ideal, Cutler Hammer, Square-D, GE, and more. You can also do an on-page external links to the product manufacturer's websites giving you even better SEO.

By doing this, you give the web crawlers another reason to rank you higher when searchers, who are dedicated to a particular brand, are looking for that brand. For example, there may be a facilities manager that has spent decades admiring the work of Siemens industrial controls. This facilities manager may be looking for an electrician that specializes in this particular brand. You want to set yourself apart and have a website page dedicated to this brand.

"Let's say that your automation and controls division only services Siemens' products. You need to have a page that showcases your work with Siemens' products."

Question 5

Do you have unique content on each of the pages of your website?

With all the hard work of creating many, many pages for your website, that is still not enough. Each page can be duplicated (there are great Wordpress plugins for page duplication ("Duplicate Page" is one but several good page duplication plug-ins to choose from) but the content must be changed according to the products or services and sometimes even the location.

If you want Google to take you serious and not look at your pages as spam, you need to create different and unique content for every page. You cannot duplicate the pages and just change out a few lines of type. You need to write the unique content based on the subject matter for each individual page. If you offer landscape lighting, talk about how you can improve the way, feel, and the mood of the lighting that enhances the landscape and architecture. Same with Industrial Automation, try to write content that will strike a chord with an engineer, plant manager, or facility manager.

Now, you have seen the importance of having individual pages, each having a different, concise H1 header. It is now time to write unique content based on each individual page. If you are having a hard time finding what to write, scour the internet for the topic of your web pages. There is plenty of information to find and you will be able to glean that information and ad the content to your individual pages. Just remember to put your spin on it to make it unique to your website. It's actually easier than you think.

When it comes to today's marketing, "Content is King". If good, quality content is "King", then long-form content is "Queen". In a late 2018 study conducted by SEMrush, long-form content that has between 1200 to 1600 words has more traffic, more social shares, and more backlinks.

As an electrician, you need to accept the fact that you need to completely understand your craft and become a subject matter expert. You may not be the best writer but you need to learn to convey your expertise in short stories to push your website to the masses.

Ideally, longer posts are better (3,000 words or a little more) because it attracts more backlinks and therefore increases your page's authority and ranking in SERPs (Google Search Results Pages). Your content should not contain "fluff". It should be high-quality, original, and relevant content that pertains to your electrical industry.

It is also practical to focus on contents that will remain useful and relevant over a long period of time. If you are the one writing a blog post or an article, try to think like the customer and what information that they would want to read. That way, the information you impart in your content will not be easily outdated and will hopefully gain a customer. Also, as you write the content, try to link certain words to pages of your website or external pages. Linking in WordPress is very easy to do. Try your best to type in keywords without interrupting the flow of the topic or without sounding like you are adding a lot of "fluff" to the article.

Quality content should be easily understood. It doesn't have to be filled with jargon, technical electrician's terminology or grandiose words that only industry professionals or lawyers could understand. Write the way that you would communicate with your customers. Try to write in short paragraphs to make your content easier to digest and use bullet points when you need to draw attention to important information within your document so that the reader can identify the key issues and facts quickly.

Content doesn't have to be written information. Content can come in a variety of forms. A simple daily/weekly post of a single picture to your Google My Business (GMB) page can do wonders in increasing your visibility on the internet. The most popular forms of content are going to be photos, articles, videos, and even audio files. As an owner of an electrical company, you need to determine what works best for you. Some people are natural writers while some are natural photographers. Others may want to leave everything to a dedicated staff member. Either way, you need to consistently add content to your website or to your Google My Business page.

We will discuss "Google My Business" (GMB) even more later in this book.

Earlier I mentioned a 2018 content study by SemRush. That same study also showed that video and great photos are almost as impressive as good, quality, long-form content. You are free to include media in your content to make it easier to understand and more entertaining to read or you can take your content and just make a video our of it. Sometimes, just seeing a video, about the content, is more understandable and digestible than reading the content.

The name of the game is "consistency". When adding content to your site, you need to be consistent and get a rhythm for adding content on a daily, weekly, or monthly basis. Remember that Google's algorithm sees activity as a good thing and thinks that "this business is open" and creating good, quality content.

Question 6

Are you helping Google understand your true service area?

Once again, Mr. Ozburn's old website was not harnessing the true power of Google. As we are building out the new website, we are trying to create a good looking site that is highly functional but more importantly, Google friendly. To be completely honest, it's all about branding your image across Google. You don't necessarily have to have a great, eye-catching site. It just needs to be the best at on-page SEO. No one really cares what your site looks like as long as it looks "somewhat professional". The people that are looking at your site are more concerned about replacing a sizzling receptacle or restoring power after the masthead was torn away during last night's thunderstorm. The most important thing about your site is that it is "findable" by the searcher. If someone is 25 miles away and needs the "best local electrician near me", your site should "pop-up" on the first page of SERP.

Our intentions are to create a site with a strong on-page SEO that search engines can easily crawl and index. At this point, early in designing and building your website, your website most-likely **does not** show up in a Google search. If you follow what is in this book, you can rectify that within 6-9 months with a strong SEO plan and even quicker using the 80-20 rule as seen on p. 71.

Here's a test for you. After a few months of incorporating some of the strategies of this book, does your website show up when someone, via a search through Google.com, types in the keywords that are important to your company?** Homework! - Have friends and family actively enter "electrical" keywords in the Google search bar looking for an electrician. Hopefully your SERP rating will get better and better as the days/months go by allowing for excellent search results from your friends and family searching. It can only happen if you do your part and are active in increasing the on-page and off-page SEO of your website.

Here are some of the things that need to be done or at least considered in order for your site to start showing up in a "Search". The first thing is to claim your Google My Business (GMB) page (See next question 7). Once you claim this, you will work with it similar to working with the content on your website. We will talk more about GMB later in answering question 7.

All of the prior information in this book, along with the following information is vital in relation to your business showing up in a potential customer's local search using the Google search bar.

A) Local Service Ads - Previously known as Google Home Services, this is a pay-per-lead service offered by Google. There is a verification process before the business is able to participate. *See the top of image on p. 126.*

B) Paid Listings (PPC Listings) - Another service offered by Google is Adwords. Adwords are a "Pay-Per-Click" service where you pay a fee every time someone clicks your ad or link. In this "pay to play" scenario, you are able to list your service(s) based on specific keywords that are relevant to your business in a specific geographical location. *See top and middle of image on p. 126.*

C) Map Listings - Don't underestimate the importance of maps being the first thing that pop up when doing a locally based search. If someone searches for "electrical repair in Atlanta", most likely a Map Listing will be the first thing they see. One important note is that there is no costs for receiving clicks to your Map Listing. This is a great way to showcase your business in a local area without the expenses of PPC. *See bottom of image on p. 126.*

D) Organic Listings - The organic section of the SERP, the search engine results pages, appears directly underneath the Map Listings in many local searches. If there is not Map Listing, the organic listings appear underneath the "Ad" or paid listings. You can differentiate the paid from the organic because the paid will have the tiny word "Ad" to the top left of a listing. <u>*See middle of image on p. 126.*</u>

The next few pages will go into more detail about how, by utilizing these four steps (Local Service Ads, Paid Listings, Map Listings, and Organic Listings), your business can have an advantage over other electrical companies when someone is doing a Google Search.

Please note that you do not have to spend a tremendous amount of money using pay-per-click (PPC), Adwords, or any paid advertising to have a successful marketing program. You must, however, put some time and energy into organic SEO growth if you do not plan on spending money on the PPC. Sorry, it's just the nature of the "internet advertising" beast.

Have you ever heard of the Google local 3-pack?

A local 3-pack is the listing of three businesses you see first in the search results when searching for terms using keywords like "electrician near me" or "near 'Your City'." When someone conducts a search for a local business, product or service, Google generates a list of potential businesses that fit the search query. At the top of the page is the Local Service Ads.

"Your goal is to be in the local 3-pack!"

The prior two pages show a local Google search for an "electrician" in the city of Covington, GA (Covington, GA is about 35 electrician   ✕ 🔍

🔍 All   ⊙ Maps   🖼 Images   📰 News   ▶ Videos   ⋮ More   Settings   Tools

About 214,000,000 results (0.56 seconds)   **Local Service Ads at the top**

10+ electricians nearby   Sponsored ⓘ

Allgood Plumbing, Ele...	Reliable Electricians -...	Gravette Electrical Se...
4.5 ★★★★★ · See reviews	4.9 ★★★★★ · See reviews	5.0 ★★★★★ · See reviews
✅ GOOGLE GUARANTEED	✅ GOOGLE GUARANTEED	✅ GOOGLE GUARANTEED
Serves Porterdale	Serves Porterdale	Serves Porterdale
(404) 736-1432	(770) 691-9296	(404) 879-6740
Open 24/7	Open 24/7	Open now

→ More electricians in Porterdale

Paid Ad (Adwords)

Ad · local.allgood-atlanta.com/electrician ▾ (404) 689-5715

Electrician - $79 Electric Panel Inspection

The **Electricians** at Allgood Can Safely Handle Any of Your Home's Electrical Issues.
Background Tested Techs. $79 Electrical Inspection. Guaranteed Warranty.
Deal: $50 off Electrical Repair · On orders over $200 · Ends Aug 31 **Map Listings (Free)**

Precision Electric Inc   Walmart Supercenter

U.S 278 NW   Ozburn Electrical
                                          Contractors Inc.

                                          Map data ©2020

Rating ▾   Hours ▾   Your past visits ▾

⚠ Hours or services may differ

Ozburn Electrical Contractors Inc.
4.9 ★★★★★ (8) · Electrician
8316 Hazelbrand Rd NE   🌐   ◈
Open · Closes 5PM · (770) 784-1618   WEBSITE   DIRECTIONS

Newton Electric Supply
4.8 ★★★★★ (27) · Electrician
8155 Hwy 278 NE · Near Ozburn Electrical Contractors Inc.   🌐   ◈
Open · Closes 5PM · (770) 786-8193   WEBSITE   DIRECTIONS

Precision Electric Inc
No reviews · Electrician   ◈
127 Hwy 81   DIRECTIONS

Ozburn Electrical Contractors Inc.

4.9 ★ ★ ★ ★ ★ (8) · Electrician

8316 Hazelbrand Rd NE

Open · Closes 5PM · (770) 784-1618

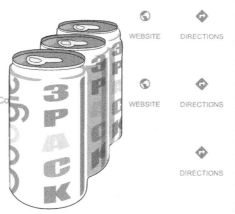

WEBSITE   DIRECTIONS

Newton Electric Supply

4.8 ★ ★ ★ ★ ★ (27) · Electrician

8155 Hwy 278 NE · Near Ozburn Electrical Co

Open · Closes 5PM · (770) 786-8193

WEBSITE   DIRECTIONS

Precision Electric Inc

No reviews · Electrician

127 Hwy 81

(770) 787-1879

DIRECTIONS

≔ More businesses

www.angieslist.com › ... › Electricians › GA › Covington ▾

Top 10 Best Electricians in Covington GA | Angie's List

Read real reviews and see ratings for Covington, GA **Electricians** for free! This list will help you pick the right pro **Electrician** in Covington, GA.

People also ask

Is being an electrician dangerous?   ⌄

Where can I find a good electrician?   ⌄

How do you calculate electrical work?   ⌄

What is the highest level of electrician?   ⌄

Organic Listings (part of your site SEO)   Feedback

ozburnelectrical.com ▾

Electrician Near Me | Electrical Contractors | Covington | Atlanta

Ozburn Electrical Contractors when it comes to high quality electrical work, It's possible that there may NOT be a more reliable and well suited then us.

www.indeed.com › Construction & Extraction › Electricians

Electrician Jobs, Employment in Covington, GA | Indeed.com

16 **Electrician** jobs available in Covington, GA on Indeed.com. Apply to **Electrician**, Industrial **Electrician**, Journeyman **Electrician** and more!

www.simplyhired.com › ... › Electricians ▾

14 Best electrician jobs in Covington, GA (Hiring Now ...

We're also looking for Licensed Journeyman **Electricians** to join our team! A Journeyman **Electrician** may lead up to 4 apprentices while installing electrical...

miles east of Atlanta, GA) and the results of Local Service Ads, Paid Listings, Map Listings, and finally Organic Listings. Ideally you want to be in the Map and the Organic Listings. If you are utilizing paid advertising, you want to also be in the Paid Listings.

The last two pages show a pretty good map listing placement and a good organic listing placement for Ozburn Electrical Contractors, Inc. (notice the Site Title and Tag Title). This would not have been possible without the proper on-page SEO and off-page SEO utilizing the proper keywords. Choosing the right keywords are crucial for getting your pages organically ranked. Let's talk about that now.

5 tips for ranking in the local SEO 3-pack
Now that we have touched on the 3-pack, do you want to see your business in the 3-pack?

Check out these tips!

1. Perform a Google search on "electrician near me" or some service that you provide.
Take a look at the SERP (page results). See if your business is in the top 15 electrical companies listed without including the paid ads.

Before you start to optimize your search engine listing, you'll want to see where you stand. It is important that you see if your business is in the top 15 for your local area or the area that you are targeting.

> **NOTE: To rank the highest in a Google Search, you must have a physical location address in the area that you service. For example, if your business's address is 1234 Mulberry Lane, Flint, Michigan, you will not naturally rank as high (organic on-page, off-page SEO) for a different city, for example, Pontiac, Michigan unless you have another physical mailing address or secondary location address (no PO Box) in Pontiac, Michigan.**

The top 15 list will change order based on your location, but the same businesses are listed. Basically, the businesses change order based on a searcher's location to your business. If you are in one of the top 15 positions, you have a good start to optimize your list.

2. Fill out your Google My Business page entirely
To understand Google My Business even more, please read more under the question 7 answer on pp. 134-137.

Notes

_____

> **"The aim of marketing is to reduce the need for selling."**
> **- Philip Kotler**

3. Get reviews on your Google profile

This is one of the most important tips in this book!

Reviews are extremely important for your business. Google's search algo-rithm now holds "reviews" in high esteem when someone performs a search query for your services. Reviews, in a nutshell, either drive traffic to local businesses or away from local businesses. People look for reviews to see if a company is worth visiting and patronizing. In fact, almost 84% of consumers trust online reviews just as much as personal recommenda-

tions.

Since reviews matter to your au-dience, you want to "legally and ethically" sway or convince your customers to leave good reviews about their experi-ence after using your company's products or services. If a customer experience was "not so good", do whatever you "legally" can to rec-tify the situation before the customer has the opportunity to leave a bad review (no, you can't give them a gift, money, etc.,). You cannot stop them from leaving a bad review. Just try to be preemptive and treat the customer like a king from the beginning. It will pay off in the long-run.

Almost 84% of consumers trust online reviews just as much as personal recommendations.

Be very careful in the way you ask customers to leave reviews about your company. You cannot offer money or other rewards for Google reviews. Google, as well as most other review sites and directories, strictly prohibit the use of money, discounts, gifts, or other rewards for reviews. *You can actually be banned if you are caught soliciting reviews in exchange for money, gifts, etc.* For Google's review policies, the exact wording is quite simple; "Contributions must be based on real experiences and information. Deliberately fake content, copied or stolen photos, off-topic reviews, defamatory language, personal attacks, and unnecessary or incorrect content are all in violation of our policy."

Here are a few tips about asking for reviews from a customer.

A) Can I ask customers for reviews? <u>Yes</u>, you can ask customers to submit reviews, but Google review guidelines forbid "soliciting reviews from customers in bulk." If you have a feeling that a customer will not leave you a "glowing" review, try to rectify the problem before asking for a review.

> *"The only way to serve your company's interest is to serve your customer's interest."* - **Philip Kotler**

B) Can I pay customers for reviews? <u>No</u>. Google and most other review sites state in their terms of service that paying for reviews is strictly prohibited and considered illegal. Google, like most review sites, does not allow the use of money, discounts, gifts, or other rewards for reviews.

C) Can I stop customers from writing bad reviews? <u>No</u>. Google review policies expressly forbid "selectively soliciting positive reviews from customers." If you have an idea or suspicion that a customer will leave a "bad" review, try to rectify the problem without mentioning the review process to them. The best solution is to do the job to the customer's satisfaction within reason.

D) Can employees post reviews? <u>*No*</u>. This is considered a "material relationship" and forbidden in the Google review guidelines. A material relationship means a familial, financial, professional or employment relationship that would impair the objectivity of the person's judgment when leaving a review.

E) Will Google delete a fake review? <u>*Unfortunately not always*</u>. You can and should respond to any negative review. You can leave a "reply" or flag it, and report the fake review. However, since it's difficult to prove on your part, fake reviews aren't usually deleted.

F) What are the consequences of not following Google review policies? <u>*BAD*</u>. Google has removed reviews and can ban users from their services.

Typically reviews can be a great enhancement to your marketing strategy. Additionally, when you earn reviews, you will boost your visibility. People will see your star rating when they see the local SEO 3-pack and be more interested in seeing what your business has to offer them.

If you have good reviews, you will attract more people to your listing. This will help your business earn more credibility and clicks to your website.

4. Sponsor events to garner local relevant links and backlinks to boost visibility.

As you already know by now, link building is a big part of SEO. You want to create as

many on-page and off-page links as possible. You can also earn links to help improve your site's ranking.

As a local business, try to earn locally-relevant links. These are links from other local businesses, non-profits, schools, institutions, etc., that drive traffic back to your business's website. It helps more people find your business.

You will earn local links by sponsoring nonprofits or sponsoring events, such as school drives, recreation sports, agriculture projects, hospital or nursing home events, and more. Leads will not only see your business's name, follow the link to your website, and learn more about your business, but these links are important metadata for search engines. This will also boost your brand recognition in the community.

The important part is that you get your business image and brand out there. You want more people to visit your business and use your services. This can lead to more "good" reviews for your business, which will help your local listing. Aside from locally relevant links, you'll also want to build backlinks. Backlinks are the most effective links to increase your website's ranking. It helps improve your website's organic ranking.

By earning backlinks, you build your business' trust and authority. This will help you build a strong Google listing, which can help you get into the SEO 3-pack.

Even if people skip the local SEO 3-pack, you'll still have a website that ranks strongly organically so leads can still find your site.

5. Build your social media presence

Social media is a great tool for local businesses. It provides you with the opportunity to connect to your local customers. You will build stronger relationships with your customers by using social media.

Your social media presence will help you improve your Google listing. If people are connecting with your business on social media, you can guide them to visit your website. This will lead to a boost in traffic, which will help improve your organic and Google ranking.

Social media helps you earn more reviews too. People can review your business on social sites like Facebook to improve your reputation. The more positive experiences leads have with your business, the more clicks your Google listing will receive.

Question 7

Have you claimed your Google My Business (GMP) page?

A good marketing agency will lead you to your Google My Business page and claim it for you. GMB is free, easy-to-use, and a necessary tool for your businesses to manage your online presence. It is not enough to have a great, SEO optimized, website. GMB is basically another version of your website that you need to use as if it were your website. If you claim, verify and edit your business information, you can both help customers find your business and tell them your story. GMB makes it easy to manage the information that Google users find when they search for your business, or the products and services that you offer.

Businesses that verify their information with Google My Business are twice as likely to be considered reputable by consumers.

Make sure to completely fill out the information about your business completely. When searchers look for your local business, they want to obtain information about it. This helps them decide if your business is the right choice for them. To rank better in the Google local SEO 3-pack, include your company's information in a business listing. Make sure to be consistent in the way that you enter your company's name. *For example, if your company is Smith Electrical Company, LLC, don't list it as Smith Electric. You have to pay attention to the details.*

Fill out your GMB listing completely so Google can gather specifics about your company. Make sure to include your updated address, contact information, and other important details.

Most importantly, make sure your hours of operation are up to date. When you add your business hours to your listing, leads see phrases such as "opens soon," "open," or "closing soon." Google My Business will also give you the opportunity to enter holiday hours, as the holiday approaches.

It's important that they see the right hours so they can visit or call your electrical business during the appropriate hours.

Potential customer need to easily have access to information like your hours, website, and

Ozburn Electrical Contractors Inc.

| Website | Directions | Save |

4.9 ★ ★ ★ ★ ★ 8 Google reviews

Electrician in Covington, Georgia

✔ You manage this Business Profile ⓘ

Address: 8316 Hazelbrand Rd NE, Covington, GA 30014

Hours: Open · Closes 5PM ▾

Phone: (770) 784-1618

Appointments: ozburnelectrical.com

Edit your business information

street address. GMB also gives customers the opportunity to leave positive reviews and post photos about your business. According to Google, businesses that add photos to their Business Profiles receive 42% more requests for directions on Google Maps, and 35% more clicks through to their websites than businesses that don't.

According to Google, businesses that add photos to their Business Profiles receive 42% more requests for directions on Google Maps, and 35% more clicks through to their websites than businesses that don't.

Another good reason to claim your GMB site is that it gives you a pretty decent analytics dashboard, both on your PC or your Smart Phone, where you can follow how leads are looking at your GMB information. By using the GMB dashboard, you can easily find insights on how customers searched for your business, and where those customers are coming from. You can also find information like how many people called your business directly from the phone number displayed on local search results in Search and

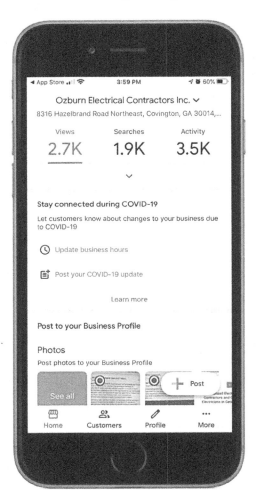

The Google My Business Phone App

Maps. When you're ready, you can create and track the performance by utilizing smart campaigns to spread the word about your business, including your work, products and services. The Google Ap makes it even easier to organize your GMB dashboard and to add content such as posts, ads, photos, and more.

Just remember, Google My Business (GMB) is free to use and it really can help your local business stand out on Google and attract new customers. Use the Google My Business app to connect with customers and keep your business presence up-to-date on Google Search and Maps.

The Google My Business app is a free mobile app making it very easy to manage your business on your smart device.

With the GMB App, you can do the following:

• Manage how your local business appears on Google Search and Maps.

• Edit your business information (e.g. address, phone number, and hours).

• Respond to reviews, questions, and messages from customers.

• Share new photos and post updates on special offers and events.

• See how customers find and interact with your business on Google.

Question 8

Does your website rank on page one for your most important keywords like "your city electrician", "your city electrical"?

Like most people, Mr. Ozburn didn't even know what a keyword was much less how to use it to improve his website's SERP ranking. His prior agency failed (probably intentionally) to mention keywords. If a marketing agency mentions or explains the term "keywords" to a customer, they then have to work harder at proving that they know what they are doing just to prove their worth.

Choosing Keywords

Keywords are those words that you think your customer will use when searching for your business. Some examples of electrical keywords are "electrician near me" or "Atlanta ceiling fan installation" or "variable frequency drives in Omaha, NE". It all depends on your target customer. If you want all new residential work, most likely you will be targeting residential general contractors. If you want residential service work, you will be targeting homeowners. There is a system to the madness. In the appendix of this book, I will provide some of the most commonly searched keywords when people need electrical services.

Here are just a few examples of electrician keywords:

1. electrician
2. electrical contractors
3. electric company near me
4. local electricians "your city"
5. licensed electrical technician

6. electrician near me
7. emergency electrician
8. journeyman electrician
9. electrical contractors near me
10. electrical contractor "your city"

On the next page I have some homework for you concerning keywords. Grab a pen and a cup of coffee and see what you can come up with for keywords for your business.

You can also download an electrician keywords form at the *www.powersurgeseo.com* website.

Long Tail Keywords

Short Tail Keywords

RIP "Murray" 2020
I miss you little guy!

Homework:

Try to list out at least ten keywords that you think relate to your business. Try to list these as though you are the ideal customer in your city looking for a particular service that your electrical business may provide. Here are a few examples:

- **"Your City" Electrician** *(obvious)*
- **Industrial PLC installation near me** *(not so obvious)*
- **Ceiling Fan Installed in "Your City"** *(not so obvious)*
- **Variable Frequency Drive repair near me** *(not so obvious)*
- **Industrial Automation "Your City"** *(not so obvious)*
- **Boat dock lights installation "Your City"** *(not so obvious)*

1) _____

2) _____

3) _____

4) _____

5) _____

6) _____

7) _____

8) _____

9) _____

10) _____

Question 9

Is your website optimized for conversion?
(turning visitors in to paying customers)

I am going to answer question 9 when I answer question 10 below.

Question 10

Do you have the Phone Number in the
top right corner on every page?

You are most likely still working diligently on your website creating new content, new pages that include great keywords. Besides having your contact information on every page, including the weekly blogs, one thing that you really need to do is make it easy for a website visitor (a potential customer or lead) to contact you as soon as possible and as conveniently as possible.

Make sure that the header of each individual page has your phone, address and contact information. In the picture top right, you can see how we utilized and maximized the phone numbers, address, clickable email address, and contact us button on the top of every page on the website. Also make sure to have your email address available and legible and just now clickable.

This, along with the Site Title and Tag Line (p. 114) is a very important step in the process of optimizing your website.

Question 11

<u>Are you using authentic images/video?</u> *Photo of the owner, photo of your trucks, photo of your team, photo of work, etc?*

It's a proven fact that people like genuine authenticity. Would you rather see real pictures of the company that you are doing business with or stock photos of someone with a brand-new tool belt, and neatly pressed and cleaned clothes with not a hint of dirt on them? I don't know about you but I would choose authenticity any day.

Try to incorporate "honest-to-goodness" real photos from real jobs and real people on your website. When it comes to videos, if a picture is worth a thousand words, a video must be worth a million! Actually the statistics prove that videos are wonderful for marketing purposes. Here's a little more information about the use of videos in your marketing plan.

Use Videos and Make Sure that They are Optimized.
Near the beginning of this book, I mentioned the importance of Google being the #1 search engine in the United States and possibly the world. Can you remember who was the #2 search engine? **Answer: YouTube**.

Here are a few little know facts about video for marketing.

• 48% of consumers want videos to reflect what they are interested in.
• 66% of video advertisements were 30 seconds long at the end of 2019.
• 66% of US teens watch online videos every day.
• 54% of all video consumers want to see more videos from brands or businesses.

YouTube is the #1 video hosting channel followed by Facebook at #2

YouTube ozburn electrical contractors inc

Ozburn Electrical Contractors, Inc. of Covington, GA 30014

Glenn Ozburn • 33 views • 1 year ago

Give Ozburn Electrical Contractors a call today at 770-784-1618 for ALL of your electrical needs! We proudly serve the entire ...

Ozburn Electrical Contractors Inc. of Metro Atlanta, Georgia (www.MrClappy.com)

Retail Marketing Graphics • 135 views • 4 years ago

Ozburn Electric is an experienced group of Certified and Licensed Electrical Contractors that are dedicated to quality and ...

Ozburn Electrical Contractors of Covington GA - 770-784-1618 - Atlanta GA and Covington GA

Get Viral! Marketing • 11 views • 1 year ago

Ozburn Electric of Covington, Georgia 30014 services the entire Southeastern United States. We have many customers in Metro ...

Ozburn Electrical Contractors - Atlanta GA

Get Viral! Marketing • 11 views • 1 year ago

Ozburn Electric specializes in every aspect of electrical services from Residential and Commercial to Industrial applications.

Ozburn Electric of metro Atlanta, GA can handle your Residential Electrical Emergencies

Get Viral! Marketing • 4 views • 1 month ago

Ozburn Electrical Contractors, Inc. not only works with Commercial Electrical and Industrial Electrical, we also offer premier ...

Ozburn Electric of Covington, Georgia (GA), metro Atlanta Electrician

Get Viral! Marketing • 4 views • 6 months ago

Ozburn Electrical Contractors, Inc. of Covington, GA is metro Atlanta, Georgia's premier electrical contractors. Ozburn Electric is a ...

A Glimpse at Ozburn Electrical Contractors, Inc.'s YouTube Video Library

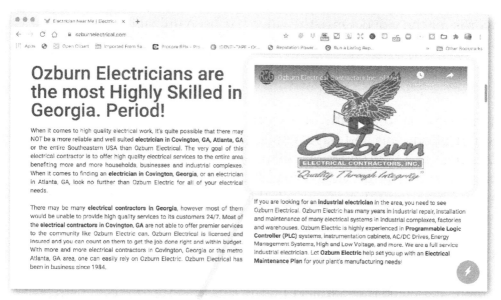

Video messages are an extremly important part of SEO. Make sure to have at least one video on the homepage of your website.

Video has continued to climb to the top of marketing and has now become a "must" for SEO marketing. Consumers are now watching more videos than ever before. It is estimated that the average person will spend 100 minutes every day watching online videos in 2021 and this will continue to grow in the years to come.

You may find video as a stumbling block but it can be turned into something fun and enjoyable. If you like to get in front of the camera, video yourself talking about a new electrical project that you are about to start or have just completed. You can also video yourself talking about some new technology that you are using (thermography, etc.,). You can video a review of a new tool or tool belt. Any thing is game when it comes to video. Just make sure to start create a YouTube channel for uploading the videos. **Keep reading to see how you can create a YouTube channel.**

Make sure that, when in the YouTube dashboard, you enter in keywords for the video. Once the video has been uploaded, you can link it to your website. This will help with On-Page and Off-Page SEO.

But how do I make a video that appeals to my customers?

I can answer that with one word, "Authenticity". Just get your smart phone out and have someone video you talking about your business and how you treat clients with the utmost respect. People love to see genuine videos that show the personal side of a company. They don't want to watch the CEO of a mega company. They want to see and hear the owner of a local business. Next, do video interviews with your workers. Make sure that everyone looks clean, nice and respectable. You can also record a video review of a particular tool or "the dangers of electricity". When it comes to video, all "electrical" subject matter is game.

A young electrician at Ozburn Electrical Contractors, Inc., liked his Klien tool pouch so much that he did an online YouTube review about it and has an astounding amount of views so far.

Once these videos are completed in this stage, you can then use some simple software such as iMovie, OpenShot, Movie Maker 10, VSDC Free Video Editor, or Wondershare to add text, logos, etc., Once this is complete, you can upload the video to your newly created YouTube Channel. Once uploaded, make sure to add the tags (keywords) in the YouTube dashboard. Once you publish the video, copy the url link to the video and place on your website, Facebook post, etc.,

But how do I create a YouTube Channel?

You can easily start your own YouTube Channel or add a business channel to your marketing plan. Create a channel with your business name or another name.

144

(A) Sign in to YouTube on a computer or your smart device.

(B) If you have already joined YouTube, go to your channel list.

(C) Choose to create a new channel or use an existing Brand Account.

A YouTube brand account is an account that is specifically for your brand. This account is different from your personal Google account. If a channel is linked to a Brand Account, multiple people can manage it from their Google Accounts. You don't need a separate username or password to manage YouTube channels with a Brand Account.

• Create a new channel by clicking "Create a new channel".

• Create a YouTube channel for a Brand Account that you already manage by choosing the Brand Account from the list. If this Brand Account already has a channel, you can't create a new one—you'll just be switched over to that channel if you select the Brand Account from the list.

(D) Fill out the details to name your new channel and verify your account. Then, click Done. This creates a new Brand Account.

Notes

I personally recommend the bulk of your videos to be in the range of 15-30 seconds. Anything longer, unless the video is extremely compelling, will be seen as too long.

 This image, top of next page, shows the YouTube video details where you can name the video and also provide a description underneath the video.

B The next picture shows the Video Analytics dashboard. When you have uploaded your video, here is where you see is the overall video performance of your channel and how popular your videos are among your target audience. With the YouTube Video Analytics, you get to measure:

- Watch time: how long are people watching my videos? How many views do I have?

- Audience retention: how consistently are people watching my videos? When are people interacting with my content? When do they stop watching?

- Demographics: who's watching my videos? What countries are my views coming from

- Playback locations: where are people actually playing my videos?

- Traffic sources: where are people discovering my videos?

- Devices: what percentage of my views come from desktop, mobile, or elsewhere?

By now you already know that Google owns YouTube. Over the last 10 years, there has been a significant increase in how much videos affect your search engine ranking or SERP.

FYI, You're 53 times more likely to show up first during a Google search if you have a video embedded on your website*.

*According to Moovly, a cloud based multimedia site, you're 53 times more likely to show up first during a Google search if you have a video embedded on your website.

(C) The following picture shows the video's "tags" or keywords that I have listed as the metadata for this video. When you upload a video in YouTube, you have the opportunity to list keywords that you think will help leads find your video.

When thinking of keywords, try to think like the customer would think. In a sense, this is similar to someone doing a search in the Google search bar. Also, in every video that you upload, make one of the keywords the same from video to video.

For example, I have put a keyword of **"OzburnElectric123!"**. Most likely this keyword will be unique to your videos whereas all the other keywords may be used in other electrician's keywords. By doing this, it will group all of your videos together. Have you ever noticed that when you are watching a YouTube video, there are other videos waiting in line for you to watch? By putting this unique keyword in your "Tags" panel, it helps to keep all of your videos grouped together thereby allowing the viewer see all of your videos as a group, playing behind one another.

Also, in every video that you upload, make one of the keywords the same from video to video. For example, I have put a keyword of "OzburnElectric123!".

Now when someone is watching a video of yours, the next video to play will most likely be another one of your videos since it has the same keyword "tag" located in the YouTube video metadata.

Notes

_____
_____
_____
_____
_____
_____
_____
_____

Question 12

Do you have a compelling Call To Action after ever blog of text?

After you have created your website, you are still not finished. You need to create a blog post once a week or at the least, once every few weeks. This blog post can be about anything related to electrical services, electricians, or anything of importance relating to the issues of the day.

Creating and writing a blog is super easy with your WordPress website. Here's a quick beginners guide on how to create a new blog post in WordPress!

Step 1: Log in to WordPress
Go to yoursite.com/wp-admin and log in with your username and password.

Once logged in, you will be taken to the WordPress dashboard. If you were already logged in, you'll go straight to the WordPress dashboard without having to log in again.

Step 2: Create a new post

There are several ways to add a new post – the easiest way is to hover over the Posts tab and click "Add New".

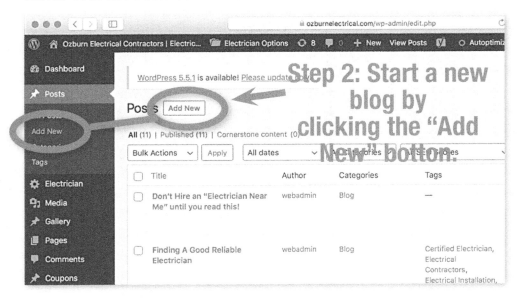

Notes

_____

_____

_____

_____

_____

_____

_____

_____

_____

_____

_____

Step 3: <u>Enter the title of your new post</u>
Put the title of your post in the first box at the top that says "Enter title here".

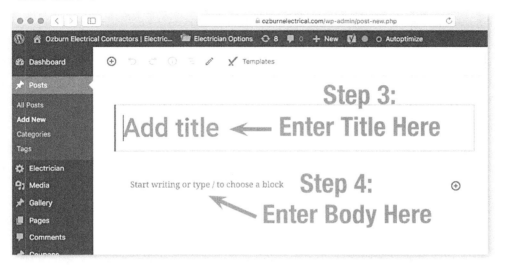

Step 4: <u>Enter body content</u>
The big box below the title box - "Start writing or type / to choose a block" - is where you put all the text, images and other content that makes up your new blog post.

Step 5. <u>Choose a feature image (See next page)</u>
The feature image will usually be shown at the very top of the post. It will also be your post's thumbnail, meaning wherever this post appears, the thumbnail image will appear along with it.

When you create your blog post, make sure to add hyperlinks throughout the post. These hyperlinks can link to internal pages on your website or external pages of citations or other website pages. Part of a good SEO strategy is a lot of links, internal and external, that lead internet surfers back to your website. Make sure that your blog posts are thoroughly thought out and well written. Google's algorithms are sophisticated enough to determine "good quality" from "bad quality".

Always take a lot of "before and after" pictures when you are on the job. Load them into your media library on your website. This will insure that you have images available to use when posting a blog.

Step 6: <u>Enter Tags</u> - When adding tags, add single keywords that apply to electrical work. Separate each keyword with a "comma" or hit the enter key and create a new keyword. Here is a short list of some suggested keywords for tags.

electrician, electrical, lighting, electric, serviceman, servicewoman, serviceperson, residentialelectric, homeelectric, commercialelectric, industrialelectric, ceilingfaninstallation, docklighting, badreceptable, christmaslights, seasonallighting, electricalcompany, electricalservices, automation, controls, vfds, plcs, assemblyline, industrialdrives, maintenanceplan, emergencyelectrician, licensedelectrician, 24hourelectrician, landscapelighting, manufacturing, facilitymanager, retailcenter, evcharger, evchargerinstallation, level2charging, FastDCcharging, plantmanager, etc.

You may have a limit to the amount of words that you can use. Pick the best 5 to 10 keywords for the post's or blog's subject matter.

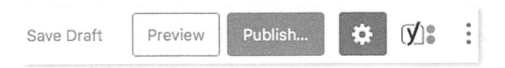

Step 7: <u>Add Categories or Go Ahead and Publish!</u> You can always add categories if you like but you can also submit your post now by clicking the "Publish" button and you're done!

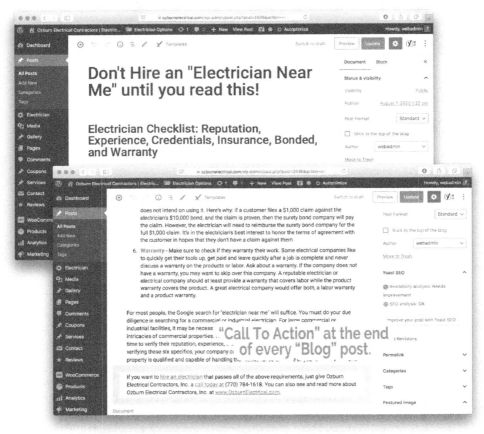

The picture above shows a blog post at OzburnElectrical.com entitled ***"Don't Hire an "Electrician Near Me" until you read this!*** At the end of the post (or article), we have a specific "Call To Action", with several hyperlinks to internal pages, contact pages, and more.

This last paragraph is the "Call To Action" to entice the reader to call now.

Here is what the last paragraph (a call to action) states:

"If you want to hire an electrician that passes all of the above requirements, just give Ozburn Electrical Contractors, Inc. a call today at (770) 784-1618. You can also see and read more about Ozburn Electrical Contractors, Inc. at www.OzburnElectrical.com."

Notes

_____
_____
_____
_____
_____
_____
_____
_____
_____
_____
_____
_____
_____
_____
_____
_____
_____
_____
_____
_____
_____

> *"Companies pay too much attention to the cost of doing something. They should worry more about the cost of not doing it."* - Philip Kotler

Question 13

Is your website MOBILE site friendly?

On April 21, 2015, Google expanded the use of mobile-friendliness as a ranking signal. This change affected all mobile searches and had (and still has) a significant impact in search results. Suffice it to say, mobile devices are not only here to stay, Google is going to put more emphasis on mobile than it does a standalone pc.

Earlier we noted that according to a CNBC article, by the year 2025, 75% of the world will only use their smartphones to access the internet. When someone has a need for electrical services, more times than not, they have their mobile device in their hand or on their body. They don't wait until they're conveniently at a computer. They search, using their smart phone, then and there. They have an electrical issue that needs to be addressed. If your website is not mobile friendly, chances are, your competition's site is. If you don't have a mobile version of your website, you could be losing potential customers.

One more note, there is a difference between "mobile friendly" and "mobile responsive". Mobile friendly simply redirects your website to a mobile optimized version of your site. A mobile responsive site is built specifically for mobile and smart devices. This is the ideal way to build your website out. Whether you go to the website on a desktop computer or from a mobile device, the site remains the same site. It just shifts to fit the screen.

Regardless of how you choose to make your site "mobile" friendly, it must be done in today's mobile centric environment.

Question 14

Are you consistently creating new content, blogging and creating new inbound links back to your website?

At this point we have covered many topics and your head is probably spinning around. That is a classic symptom of "Marketing Anxiety". It's ok and we are still here to help you at help@ powersurgeseo.com.

Now back to the question.

Are you consistently creating new content, blogging and creating new inbound links back to your website?

By this time, you should probably have your website up and running but working on it daily; perhaps a little fine-tuning.

When it comes to new content or blogging, you need to be thinking of *"what is going on in the electrical services world that would persuade someone to find interest in your services through a blog or newsletter?"* Maybe articles about ceiling fan installation, GFI receptacles, Assembly line automation or ev charger upgrades. The subject matter is unlimited in the electrical services industry.

Even though the subject matter is unlimited, blogging or creating content can still be one of the toughest jobs to do if you don't like to write. You can always find others to write the material for you. Go to sites like fiverr.com or upwork.com to hire someone to write "electrical services" content for you. If you do take this option, please make sure to read the final written materials thoroughly and approve before paying. One thing that I have noticed when outsourcing blogs, newsletters, social media, etc., is the fact that no one except you and your local community know the "jargon" or "vernacular" for your community or region of the country. Because of this, you often get poorly written articles and blogs that really don't make sense and ironically, they hurt you in the long run. Case in point. **Have you ever seen an item manufactured in another country and the instructions don't make any sense?** It's most likey because the foreign country doesn't know the english language that well but they also have to know the english "slang" language and territorial vernacular.

Make sure to go over the content thoroughly and rewrite if you have to. You want the final content to sound as though you wrote the material, yourself, to your customer base. Finally, make sure that you upload the content as a blog post to your WP site. This way you can add internal and external links and pictures. **If you do write a blog post yourself, make sure to use compelling language and insert internal and external hyperlinks (see pictures on the next page) throughout the post.**

This leads up to the next sub-section of…

Use Descriptive and SEO-Friendly URLs.

For example, when compelling a website visitor to look at your page about EV Charging on the Ozburn Electric website, we have the following style URL.

https://ozburnelectrical.com/ev-charger-installation-chargepoint-installer-georgia-ga/

This url is broken up with hyphens and that is what Google

Here is an example of applying an internal or external link in a post or a blog. This same principle applies to other aspects of WordPress.

To add an internal or external link, highlight the word...

With the word highlighted, click on the "Link" button above in the tool bar.

This window will then open up and you can either type or paste an internal or external link in the top line.

159

likes. It basically adds to the on-page SEO by telling search engines that the page is about EV (electrical vehicle) charger installation in Georgia. We could have entered in a shorter URL such as https:// ozburnelectrical.com/ev-charger/ but we wanted to add as much SEO information as possible in the URL. Do not use special characters in your URL and in most cases, try to keep it short, around a maximum of 5-7 words.

Have a Compelling Meta Description.

The Meta Description, as seen below, may not be that compelling but when you have many pages in a website, try to change the Meta Descriptions slightly one from another. The "Yoast" plugin is an excellent WordPress plugin for adding Meta Descriptions to your website pages.

 ozburnelectrical.com

Electrician Near Me | Electrical Contractors | Covington | Atlanta

Ozburn Electrical Contractors when it comes to high quality electrical work. Metro Atlanta, GA's best electricians ready to service your electrical needs.

An example of Meta Descriptions; here the small snippet of text that best describes your page's content on the SERP.

Use Subheadings and Header Tags.

Include subheadings in your content (next page framed and highlighted in yellow). Doing so will give you the opportunity to include your keywords in your content thereby possibly giving you a better SERP rating while also a better user experience for the website visitors.

This will also make your content visually easier to scan. Since people nowadays don't have the patience to read through your article, subheadings serve, not only as roadmaps, but as keywords that will help your readers and web crawlers get an overview of your content and find the information they need easily. Remember to

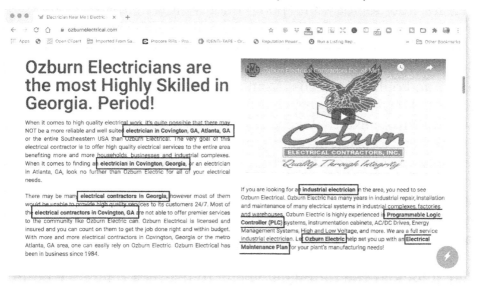

divide your content into logical and scannable chunks, preferably the keywords, that can be easily digested by your readers

Creating Links

When you are building out your website pages, remember to include internal and external links. For instance, you may list many different services that you offer. Each one of the services should have a page of it's own. Make sure to "highlight" each of the "service" words (industrial electrician, ev charger installation, residential electrician, low voltage landscape lighting, panel upgrades, etc.,) and link them to the individual pages that you have built for each service. Also, there are many ways to create external links. You can leave comments on product manufacturer pages and utilize your website address. You can create "Press Releases" with links that trace back to your website. You can blog and hope that others read your blogs and "share" your blogs. You can hire others via www.fiverr.com or www.upwork.com to create "Backlinks" and "Linkwheels" for you (pp. 45-46).

Be careful in the external links that you have to link with your website. You do not want "poor" quality sites linking back to your website. *FYI, nefarious sites are not good for business!*

Google's latest algorithm changes were aimed at preventing marketers and online specialist from abusing backlink authority. Back in the old days (a few years ago), SEO specialist could purchase backlinks from external websites and it would actually rank your site higher. Google and other search engine sites considered this not only fair but considered this as bad, irrelevant links. Now if you do anything similar to this, it can actually hurt your site. **You can go to www.fiverr.com or www.upwork.com but please make sure to select individuals that have very good reviews in doing this type of work.**

Take a look at the following visual to use as a reference point for linking opportunities.

Be sure to check out the following for more linking opportunities.

1) <u>Create interesting content and articles about your industry through the use of blogs.</u> This is probably going to be your #1 source for inbound links. You can write an article and "push" it out using Facebook, Facebook Business Page, LinkedIn, Twitter, Instagram, Pinterest, and many other free directory sites. Once you push your blog out, each one of these external sites will then contain a link back to a specific page on your site.

2) <u>Directory Listings</u> - Get your site listed on as many directory sites as possible. Some of these are free and some you may have to pay for (some of the pay sites offer free listings). These are sites like Angie's List, Yelp, Citysearch, Manta, Yellow Pages, Google My Business (GMB), Yahoo Local, Judy's Book, and more. <u>Here is a list of a few more directory sites worth giving a shot.</u>

https://botw.org

https://aboutus.com

http://www.spoke.com

https://www.blogarama.com

https://www.yellowpages.com

https://www.bingplaces.com

https://smallbusiness.yahoo.com/local

http://business.foursquare.com

https://www.chamberofcommerce.com

https://www.hotfrog.com

https://www.merchantcircle.com

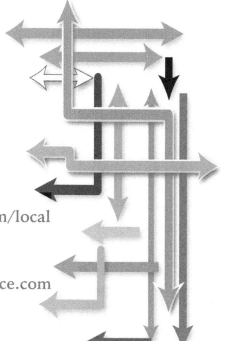

https://www.bbb.org

https://www.superpages.com

https://nextdoor.com

https://www.elocal.com

https://www.dexknows.com

https://www.alignable.com

https://www.local.com

https://www.b2byellowpages.com

> In the Appendix of this book, you will find many directories sites listed to join and add your business. Please remember to write down the user-name and password in the noted areas. You will need your login information for any changes.

3) <u>Association Links</u> - Be sure that you have a link from any industry association page that you belong to. If you belong to the Independent Electrical Contractors, ask them to post your infor-mation on their site. If you belong to the Chamber of Commerce, once again, have them post your information on their site. You can do this with the Better Business Association, any Civic Orga-nizations, Networking Groups, and more.

4) <u>Ask Around</u> - You can work with friends and colleagues that have affiliated or similar sites in the electrical services industry. You can ask electrical product manufacturers or electrical supply houses if they will post a link to your website on their site and you can offer to do the same for them. If you do a lot of resi-dential electrical services, team up with realtors or real estate companies or even hardware/supply companies. Utilizing your resources and teaming up with relevant companies will add more authority to your domain.

30% of SEO is considered "on-page" SEO. The remaining 70% of SEO is considered "off-page" SEO. This very important SEO builds authority, citations and links out-side of your website.

Question 15

Do you understand the importance of NAP...
name, address, and phone number?

One of the most effective ways to generate on-page and off-page SEO for your local business, is to essentially "localize" your business across the internet. To be completely honest, the majority of people like to do business with local companies. What this essentially means is that you want your business listed in local directories but you also want your business listed in online "authority" directories. Examples of authority directories include Yellow Pages, HomeAdvisor, Yelp, Angies List, Thumbtack, BBB, Foursquare, and many others. In the SEO world these directory listings are also called Citations which Google, Bing, and other search engines use to help determine which sites are of value, and consequently which sites will rank higher than others.

Google looks at the quality of the Citations (Local Directories in our case), the quantity of quality Citations, but also the consistency of Citations. The keyword here is "consistency". This is why I am pushing you to have your name, address, and phone number consistent and used only by your business. When I mention consistency, your listings should basically be identical across the internet.

I cannot tell you how many times I come across companies whose NAP is inconsistent at best. One directory site may have a phone number of "X", and on another directory site the phone number is listed as "Y". This also applies to addresses and business's names. Some of these are common "fat finger" mistakes or just not paying attention. In some cases a hired "agency" or "SEO" company simply may not have the best interest of the company and is just listing as fast as they can to quickly satisfy their duty of supplying citations cheaply and quickly.

NAME

At the beginning of this book on p. 22, I had you list your "legal company name" and your "common company name". To understand the difference, here is an example:

Legal Company Name = Ozburn Electrical Contractors, Inc.
Common Company Name = Ozburn Electric

Early in the stages of your marketing strategy, you need to determine how you would like your company name stated on your website and across the internet. The sole purpose of this is "consistency" for better SEO. Google's algorithm is looking for your business to be consistent or it may see it as several different businesses. If you are not consistent with your name, Google may see this.

Ozburn Electrical Contractors, Inc
Ozburn Electric
Ozburn Electrical Services
Ozburn's Electrical
Ozburn's Electric Company....so forth and so on!

Try to stay consistent with your name but this is not a Google deal breaker. Google triangulates the data it finds on the web by three data points: name, address, and phone number. If two of these are a match, and then the name is a partial match, Google will have no problem associating those citations with the correct listing in GMB. As long as the phone number and address stay the same, it will have no negative impact on their rankings.

That being said, I personally would prefer that you settle upon a single name to use in your marketing strategy. That doesn't make it's wrong to use the various "slang" versions of your name. It just makes it easier for a marketing agency. Marketers like consistency across the internet for the sole purpose of on-page and off-page SEO.

ADDRESS

Also on p. 22, I had you list your physical Address. As with your name, the physical address (not a P.O. Box) is important as well. Your physical address needs to be consistent across the internet. If you have multiple locations, that is even better. When it comes to NAP, Google sees your Name, Address, and Phone number and the three totalled equal verification, or a verified "real, live" business.

NAP Stands For
Name + Address + Phone
=Verification

Google likes to see consistency in Name, Address, and Phone number. This way it tells Google that you are an actual "living, breathing" business.

When it comes to your address, have one corporate location that is the center of activity for your business. This must be an actual physical address and not a P.O. Box. It is ok to have multiple addresses. If you do have multiple, physical addressed locations, this makes it even better for SEO purposes.

PHONE NUMBER

The Phone Number is actually very important as well. By providing a real phone number, you are telling Google that you are a single business that is alive and well and accepting new customers daily. It is ok to have multiple phone numbers but for the sake of a good SEO strategy, try to list a single phone number for your citations and directories. Also another important note is to not let another business use your phone number. If you have multiple businesses such as an Electrical company, an HVAC company and a Carpet Cleaning company, do not use the same phone number. This causes problems with Google's algorithm that it trying to verify your company as a "real, live" company. Just as in addresses, it is important to distinguish each company one from another. If you have the same address for every company, each company must be legally registered as distinct entities. It is not as easy as having a different Suite number. **Google does not recognize Suite numbers!** If you have several businesses, try to use a different phone number for each business.

If you think that you can outsmart Google by having several businesses at the same address by using a Suite number, you're wrong. Google does not recognize Suite numbers!

If Google's algorithm sees multiple businesses using the same address or phone number, it may perceive it as an illegitimate company or companies. As with humans, a red flag is thrown up as to the validity of a company. With Skype, Anveo, or any other myriad of VOIP and cell options, getting another number is a dirt cheap cost for someone running a legitimate business.

In a much more real sense, your name should reflect your business' real-world name, as used consistently on your storefront, website, stationery, and as known to customers. Accurately representing your business name helps customers find your business online and through relevant search results.

When filling out information for your Google My Business, it is important to only use your real name, address and phone number. For example, if you were creating a listing for a 24 hour electrician in downtown Los Angeles called Don's Electrical Services, you would enter that business information as:

Business name: Don's Electrical Services
Address: 1234 Ridgeway Street, Los Angeles, CA 90019
Hours: Open 24 hours
Category: Electrician

Including unnecessary information in your business name is not permitted, and could result in your listing being suspended.

According to Google My Business rules, use a precise, accurate address and/or service area to describe your business location. P.O. boxes or mailboxes located at remote locations are not acceptable.

When two or more companies are using the same NAP, their Google Local listings could merge, mixing up their data and adversely affecting each business' ability to rank. Moreover, if the two businesses are sharing a phone number, I'm assuming that they have some sort of call center that's trying to divvy up calls for one business or the other and Google expects each individual business to be directly contactable at its local number. Oh what a tangled web we weave...

Website and phone
Google has this to say about websites and phone numbers... "Provide a phone number that connects to your individual business location as directly as possible, or provide one website that represents your individual business location."

Google doesn't stop there. Google, when talking about phone numbers, says to "use a local phone number instead of central, call center helpline number whenever possible. Do not provide phone numbers or URLs that redirect or "refer" users to landing pages or phone numbers other than those of the actual business, including pages created on social media sites. The phone number must be under the direct control of the business.

Additional phone numbers *can be used* on Google My Business websites and other local surfaces but premium-rate telephone numbers are not allowed. These phone numbers charge high rates to the caller" and that is what Google doesn't like.

Question 16

Do you know the Login Username and Passwords for every website or service used by your business?

When this question was asked to Mr. Ozburn, owner of Ozburn Electrical Contractors, Inc., he knew a few of the logins but only for the more familiar email address and websites. Fortunately for him, he didn't have to remember many usernames or passwords because he did not have a marketing plan to begin with.

It is vital to remember the websites or services that you have become a member of. You need to know the login information for each one. If you have to, delegate this responsibility to someone else that is considered a highly responsible person on your team. In the Appendices (p. 230) of this book, you will find an area to list your login information, site name followed by username and password. Utilize this "written" database for future use. There are many smartphone apps out there that can do the same thing but some find them cumbersome as well. One easy way to rectify this is to open up your "notes" on your smartphone and utilize this for login information. Do this only if you have a password protected phone.

Suffice it to say, it is very important for you to know your login information, if not for you, for the marketing agency working on the marketing for your business.

Here are a few tips about login usernames and passwords.

• Use random passwords, and use a different password for every site
• Use a password manager to make creating and remembering passwords easier
• Make your answers to security questions just as strong as your passwords
• Use "two-factor authentication" wherever you can
• Pay attention to the browser's security signals, and be suspicious

You can use a password manager like 1Password, LastPass, or Dashlane to help improve your password's strength. These password managers can generate strong passwords for you, remember them for you, and fill them into websites so you don't have type them in. It is worth every penny to have one of these handy when you need it.

Question 17

Does your address(es) represent an actual office space, a virtual office space, or a shared office space within an office space used by other businesses?

We basically covered the importance of "addresses" when we discussed NAP in question 15. **You can still get away with sharing businesses using the same address.** You just have to do it smart and each company must be legally registered as distinct entities and use a precise, accurate address and/or service area to describe your business location. Google doesn't take this lightly so in my opinion, it is better to have a distinct way to tell your business from other businesses. You can find out more by researching for "Guidelines for representing your business on Google".

Question 18

Is your business located in your home? If so, do you use your home's physical address for your business's physical address? Do you have a Post Office Box number?

I know that you are probably thinking, "why is this guy so adamant on addresses and this NAP thing?!"

In the last few questions, we have answered a lot of this subject matter ad nauseam. I am just trying to drive home the fact that you can save yourself and your company a lot of grief by having a completely independent NAP from any other entity or company.

There is not an official summary or guideline that forbids listing multiple service area businesses such as electricians, blacksmiths, and plumbers at the same location, *but it is not considered the industry's best practice.* Google appears to be more active in issuing suspensions to service area businesses in this situation, even if the businesses are distinct and legitimate. ***Because of this, it's better not to co-locate service area businesses.***

To be more distinct and to maybe put this matter to bed, you can have multiple businesses operating from the same location. If each co-habitating business you operate or you operate alongside another business is registered separately with the appropriate state and federal agencies, has its own unique tax ID which you file separate taxes with and meet face-to-face with customers with a unique phone number, then it is generally eligible for a distinct Google My Business listing. If you decide to do your own thing and take the chances, that is your right, but...

You may be penalized! Google could issue a hard suspension on one or more of your listings at any time.

If you get a hard suspension, it means that Google has removed your listing and its associated reviews. This will not only affect your search engine rankings, it becomes a hard task to get resolved with Google. These same type of penalties are basically across the board with other social media outlets as well. Facetime, Twitter, Instagram, etc., all have their "jail" sentences so be very careful and read all the rules.

Now, back to the question!

• Is your business located in your home? Do you use your home's physical address for your business's physical address?

Google has different rules that apply to residential as compared to a business address. There can only be two businesses per residential address and still be acknowledge by GMB.

• Do you have a Post Office Box number?".

Google My Business <u>does not</u> recognize Post Office Boxes. If it did, everyone business would have a remote location in every major city across America. Google specifically states that your business must "use a precise, accurate address and/or service area to describe your business location. P.O. boxes or mailboxes located at remote locations are not acceptable."

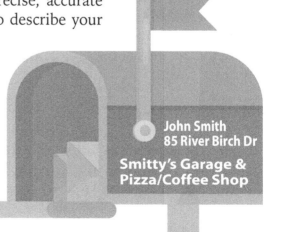

Question 19

Have any of your listed locations moved in the past 10 years? If so, please list any known former addresses or phone numbers.

Mr. Ozburn's electrical business has moved a lot over the years but not in the last 10 years. There are several reasons for moving, from company growth to moving to a more desirable location, and more. If your business moves, you need to update as much online information and you can think of. One of the first things to do is to update your address in Google My Business. This allows old and new customers to be able to visit your new location. Do not just create a new business address if you've moved from one location to another but rather delete the old address. Google may require you to verify your new business address once you update it.

Once you've updated your address, you can enter your opening date and promote your new location via posts.

If you are just starting to market your electrical services business and realize that you have duplicate locations, you can remove these old and unused locations. If you mistakenly created a new listing for your business's new address and now have two verified listings for the business (one listing for the old address, and one listing for the new address), contact Google support to remove the duplicate listing.

If for some reason you are having problems trying to remove your old location on Google, contact Google support. Google's support team can mark the business listing for your old location as "moved".

To contact Google support, go to support.google.com.

Question 20

<u>Are any other phone numbers, whether call tracking, toll free, local, or vanity being used to represent your business locations or any other type business at your location? Please list and explain.</u>

After digging a little deeper with Mr. Ozburn, we discovered that he had several phone number associated with his business. Besides the main number that he had been using since 1984, he had a few legacy phone numbers that represented areas nearby but under a different area code. I say "legacy" numbers because these numbers were basically relics of the "Yellow" pages days when it was necessary to have a phone number representing every nearby zip code. Ozburn Electrical Contractors, Inc. also has a "toll-free" line. After further discussion, Mr. Ozburn wanted to keep all of these "old" numbers for his business because some customers had grown attached to them.

Here is some advice when it comes to multiple business phone numbers.

When building out your website, you do need to use a LOCAL number that is your most commonly used phone number. Some would argue that you <u>do</u> need a "toll-free" number as well. In the old days, prior to today's emphasis on a strong SEO marketing plan, I would have agreed that you do need a toll free number. My suggestion now is that you don't need a toll free number and in fact, it may even hurt you for SEO rankings.

Some directory sites do not accept toll-free lines as primary phone numbers. Choosing a local phone number may also be better for rankings and increase the number of calls you get from local search customers.

As far as I know, Google does not forbid toll free numbers, but I would still avoid using them if possible, because of the following:

1) People like dealing with local companies. A local area code number is a signal of 'localness', just like a zip code. You always want to appear as local as possible.

2) The SEO marketing software company, Moz, found that "listing a 1-800 number as the only phone number on the Google My Business Page to be the 16th most negative ranking factor" for potential customers performing an quiry through the Google search bar. Over the years, 1-800 numbers have become suspect and have gained relatively negative opinions. This "Moz" study factor does not speak to having a 1-800 as your primary number and local as secondary, but still, there is still some perception out there as toll free numbers being negative.

3) Finally, unless your business is mail-order, hospitality, or marketing (selfish plug - haha) I don't believe that using an 1-800 number could be beneficial and it may potentially make you less powerful than competitors who are using a local number.

So, in a nutshell, if the majority of your client base has a local area code phone number, stick to having a local area code phone number yourself. On the other hand, if you've got a national customer base or have an e-commerce website, you may want to consider getting a 1-800 phone number or even a vanity number.

Thank you for calling *1-800-We-WireU*. We realize that you are 754 miles away but we will send someone out ASAP to hang that ceiling fan up for you!

Multiple Local Numbers

If you have multiple local numbers that represent different local zip or area codes, this is ok but only if you choose the most commonly used number to be your "marketing" phone number.

Ozburn Electrical Contractor, Inc., has had the same phone number, (770) 784-1618, since 1984. They also have several other "local" numbers but this is the "go-to" phone number. It is ok to have other phone numbers that represent nearby area codes but for the purposes of marketing your business, please pick one and go with it. This number needs to be placed on every page of your website and used for citation and directory listings.

You can use the other numbers on business cards, and to compliment the main number but when it comes to online digital marketing, Google needs to see only one phone number to triangulate the NAP of your business. It's just that important!

Question 21

How long has the website existed at this domain, and have there been previous domain names in the past 10 years?

When asked this question, Mr. Ozburn let us know that he had previously had the domain www.ozelec.com and was presently using www.ozburnelectric.com (notice electric and not electrical). Years ago Ozburn Electrical Contractors, Inc. had started as www.ozelec.com basically to have a shorter domain name, supposedly making it easier to type for clients and potential new customers. In my opinion, this is basically not needed because once you type the domain or web address once, it tends to populate itself the next time making it easier for those to type it in a second time. More importantly though is who usually goes to a website the second time? Usually for electricians and electrician websites, the customer finds you and really doesn't have a need to go back to the website a second time, hence the importance of creating a website that has more SEO "brawn than beauty."

Mr. Ozburn had then hired a marketing agency that had morphed over the years from a phone book into an agency. If you have been around enough years, you probably remember the importance of being in the phone book but you also remember their exorbitant fees and lack of customer support. Suffice it to say, this company had created a "Free" website for Mr. Ozburn's electrical company and it was minimalist at best. A lot of marketers will offer you a "free" website based on doing the service work and peripheral marketing work that surrounds your company and your website. Beware, if a website is free, there is usually either a catch to it or you are going to get a useless, basic site. My company, Power Surge SEO will create a site with all of the bells and whistles similar to what you see at Mr. Ozburn's electrical site (www.OzburnElectrical.com). What we expect from the customer is the peripheral marketing that surrounds the site. It is basically a "win, win" for both the customer and PowerSurgeSEO.

I digress, now back to the question about how many years that you have had your domain.

In marketing circles, there's an old saying *"that the more extended amount of time your site has established a presence online, the more it has become a trusted site among search engines and valid among visitors searching within your niche."* Is this true or just an old wives' tale? Well, in my personal opinion, there may be a hint of merit to this saying.

If you have an "older" website, let's say 5 to 10 years old, and you have put a tremendous amount of marketing effort into it, the saying will probably ring true. Your old site may have garnered enough organic SEO over the years to be crawled and indexed by all of the search engine robots out on the internet. You may have even gotten a loyal customer following out of your old website.

Does that mean your old site is still good?

It depends. If you are an e-commerce site doing a lot of online business, you probably want to keep the internal mechanism of the site pretty much the same. Maybe a quick spit shine and a new coat of digital wax. I say that because you have probably built up a tremendous amount of organic SEO that is relying on metadata, site titles and tag lines, hyperlinks and more to exist. If you decide to rebuild your website now, builder beware! If you do redesign your website, you risk losing everything that you have built, in terms of organic SEO, by dismantling the links and the "good stuff" that is in your website. If you are doing an amazing amount of online sales, my advice would be to try to keep the pages intact but maybe "spiff" them up a little with new pictures, new blog posts, and superficial changes like that. If not, you risks losing what your customer base is already accustomed to looking at.

On the other hand, if your site is your basic "run of the mill" site that is 1-10 years old or older, it would probably make sense just to start over, redesign, and rebuild. The reason that I recommend this route is the fact that when you build your page out, you need to refer back to the "marketing pyramid" and start with a great foundation. That foundation needs to be build with a strong SEO plan in mind. The web designer needs to incorporate on-page SEO and after they are finished, they need to

Does your website need to be put in the "Old Website's Home"?

179

turn it over to another SEO expert to continue and refine the SEO on the website. It is easier to tear down an existing site with a terrible foundation and start over with a new site than it is to try to rebuild the original site.

You also need to understand that a domain name's registration age has nothing to do with the site's viability. A domain/site could be 10 years old and if it's never been touch with content or indexed, it's basically at the same playing level as the newly created domain you purchased this morning. Domain age is really only important if you have been actively working the website over the years. Most businesses will have a website created or build and not touch if for years. They have fallen under the marketer's spell of "if you build the site, they will come."

If you already have a site but have not worked with it over the years, seriously consider redesigning your site to modern standards and incorporating a new marketing strategy that is based on a strong organic SEO foundation.

Notes

_____

_____

_____

_____

_____

_____

_____

_____

_____

_____

_____

_____

Question 22

<u>Please list out all of the major services and/or products that your company offers.</u>

Prior to my company working on OzburnElectrical.com, the site was your basic site. It was very plain and had no reason to compel anyone to visit and much less browse the site. The importance of a website for selling yourself and your company cannot be overstated. By having an online presence through your website, you are able to reach more consumers. The more consumers you reach online, the more opportunities you have to make a sale. It stands to reason that you have spent a fair amount of money to have your website created, **why not list all your services or products on your website?**

By writing down your services and products, you are giving them an identity. Writing them down will also give you the opportunity to really clarify what you do want to offer to your customer base. Do you want to do industrial electrical work? Do you want to offer 24/7 emergency services? Do you want to install Electric Vehicle Chargers? Do you want to install landscape lighting? Do you want to work on programmable logic controllers? The questions can be endless. You need to put pen to paper and determine what it is that you want to offer your customer. Once this is determined, you then need to either create your website based on these findings or revamp your website to match your products and services.

Your website is the backbone of your electrical business, supporting all of your products and services and you need to have a page for every product and service. Not only is this good for your business and for your potential customers to see, it provides excellent SEO benefits as well.

For an excellent example of showcasing your products and services, visit www.OzburnElectrical.com and see the multitude of pages that were created for the purpose of showing and explaining what you offer to your customer base. When at www.OzburnElectrical.com, browse over the page categories like commercial, industrial, residential, and more. Get a feel for all of the services that are offered at this single website.

Although it is nice to be able to offer so many services, don't think that your company has to offer so many services. You may want to only offer alarm system installation or industrial automation. If you do, try to find out the many varieties of alarm systems/ industrial automations and apply that to your website. There are over 100 pages at the www.OzburnElectrical.com site but you may only want 10, 20 or at the most 30 pages and that's ok. Just make sure to utilize every page to the fullest with the most up-to-date current information.

Notes

Question 23

Are you active, in any way, on social media? Personal or Business?

When it comes to social media, it seems like a never ending quest to get your company's brand or message out to the masses. You have so many different avenues to take...LinkedIn, Facebook, Instagram, YouTube, Twitter, and more!

Most business owners (especially baby boomers), have a hard time realizing the importance of social media. Even if you do realize the importance of social media, where do you start and with which social media platform do you start with?

We have spoken about "Repeat and Referral" business. It's what we like to call "word of mouth" business. **Back prior to the internet, this was your first type of social media.** All you are doing now is harnessing the power of "word of mouth" through the internet. Social media is a super powerful way of taking your "word of mouth" to the next level.

At the moment there are 1.69 billion worldwide users on Facebook. To put that in perspective, there are only 331 million citizens in America. That's like saying that there are almost 6x more Facebook users worldwide than there are citizens in America. Here are a few more amazing stats about Facebook.

56% of US citizens over 65 are on Facebook.
81% of adults in America have Facebook accounts.
71% of Americans use Facebook as a whole.

Now you see the importance of social media!

As an electrical company, you need to setup business pages for your company under the social media avenues that you feel would enhance your electrical business. If you are striving to get more residential business, you may want to consider utilizing Facebook more. If you are working on realizing more retail or commercial customers, you may want to step it up with LinkedIn. If you want to advertise more toward a younger, more hip crowd, maybe Instagram or Snapchat will be your answer. Regardless, you need to realize that the modern day "repeat and referral" is the internet and more specifically "social media."

Question 24

Are you leveraging email marketing?
(MailChimp, AWeber, Constant Contact, Sendinblue.com, ActiveCampaign.com, MailerLite.com, HubSpot.com etc.,)

When it comes to this question, we are not talking about sending one or two emails from your outlook or gmail account. We are talking about a list of prior customers or potential customers who have opted in to receiving newsletters, coupons, deals, and more from your company.

Do you have a strategy in place where you are collecting information from your customers or potential clients (leads)? It could be as simple as a "Customer Feedback Form" as seen on p. 73 or as advanced as sales funnels that are initiated from clicks on your website. Regardless, you need to be collecting as much information from your customer as possible without being too obtrusive. Make sure that your employees collect the name and email address of every person that calls into your business. If possible, even ask for permission (opt-in) to send information via text messaging to their cell phones.

Once you get all of this information, try to be consistent in sending out a monthly newsletter to each and every customer utilizing an email service such as **Constant Contact, AWeber, Sendinblue, ActiveCampaign, MailerLite, HubSpot.com or MailChimp**. In the big scheme of things, these companies are relatively low-cost for the services that they provide. Some of these companies offer a very rudimentary "free" plan but all usually offer a decent plan from $10-$20 a month. These plans give you the opportunity to upload an excel or csv file with all of your contacts or manually enter the names yourself. Once the names are populated into the

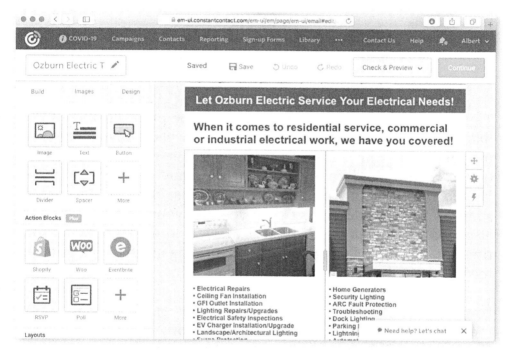

service, you will have the ability to create nice looking, professional email newsletters and send them out on a monthly basis.

Another fantastic opportunity to send an email is immediately after the service has been performed. You can send the customer an email to see how the service was performed and ask for the customer to leave you a review. We have talked about the importance of getting reviews and this is one of the best ways to get a review. You can also send an email to a recently serviced customer requesting them to seek you out on social media. This is a great way to have your customers seek out your social media and possibly get a "like" and a "share" out of it. Like we said, today's social media is like the old "repeat and referral".

All in all, email marketing is one of the least expensive ways to market your business. It is a low cost way to stay in contact with your customers and also take your business to the next level.

Question 25

Are you sending out monthly newsletters either print or email?

This question may seem redundant from the prior question but I like to be thorough to basically find out all aspects of your marketing (digital or print). There are still those rare cases where someone is creating and printing a newsletter and sending it via the United States Postal Service. I'm not against this and encourage some sort of interaction between you and your customer base. I also encourage using your money wisely and it may now be the time to go all digital when it comes to sending newsletters, printed media, or whatever via the postal service.

I would encourage you to look into various other "digital" ways to send media to your customers. Check out AWeber, Constant Contact, MailChimp, and many more companies that specialize in marketing via email.

Notes

_____

_____

_____

_____

Question 26

Are you taking advantage of Pay-Per-Click (PPC) or Pay-Per-Lead (PPL) or any other type paid online advertising?

This is a subject that we haven't discussed much yet but will talk more about now. The reason that we haven't talked about PPC or PPL much is the fact that you have to get everything else in order before you should think about "paid online advertising". When utilizing the "Marketing Pyramid" (see p. 60), we must first stive to make the website the foundation of your success. As you can see in the abbreviated version of the pyramid below, PPC is on the fifth layer while PPL is settled in at number ten. Once you get the first four levels instituted and going well, you can then decide if you want to participate in paid online marketing. I am a strong believer in organic SEO as seen in level 2. I think that one of the first thing that needs to be done after the website is strong on-page SEO and off-page SEO. The on-page SEO can be done fairly easily on your own or by the agency or person that is creating your website. The

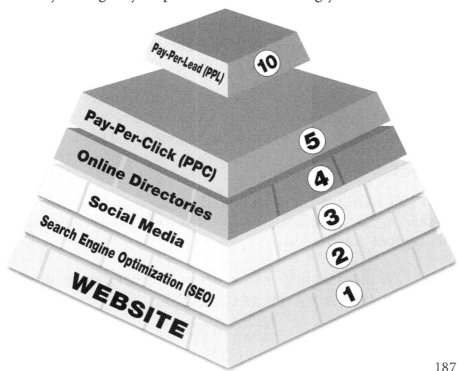

off-page SEO is a little tougher and you may need to enlist the help of a marketing agency such as Power Surge SEO or someone that specializes in on-page and off-page SEO. If you are trying to save some money, you can get help from sites such as fiverr.com or upwork.com. Make sure to search for the term "SEO" and also make sure that the person(s) have excellent ratings. Do not try to purchase SEO off of sites like eBay or similar sites. By doing this, you may be walking into nefarious individuals that may do more harm than good. When enlisting the help of others for SEO help, you will have to give login information for your website and possibly other sites. Please make sure that you have this information handy to help expedite and streamline the process.

Our company, www.PowerSurgeSEO.com, excels in everything noted in this book. If you need it done, we can do it and more. We specialize in helping electrical contractors and electricians manage their internet marketing, their print media marketing, and much more. We will design, develop and setup your website, making sure that it is optimized for SEO (search engine optimization), write content for you, blog for you, manage your social media for you, develop your website's authority over the internet via citations and directories, link build, review management, reputation management, track your online rankings, and more.

We will basically put the strategies outlined in this book into action for you and your business with minimal interaction on your part. If you need any help, just contact us at help@powersurgeseo.com.

Now back to PPC!

Once you have the foundation and the next three layers of the pyramid in place, it may make sense for you to budget for pay-per-click or even pay-per-lead.

Here is a little more information about PPC before you dive in to it too deep. **Here are a few of the CONS.**

1) PPC is extremely costly in the long run. Do you remember at the start of this book when I explained about a doctor who was spending $8,000 a month in PPC but barely getting any business? The doctor/owner talked to the agency (named after a poisonous arachnid with a long tail) and asked them what did they suggest? **Drumroll please...**

They suggested that she needed to spend another $2,000 a month on PPC. She tried that and still didn't get any business. I say that to let you know that PPC can be extremely expensive and the fact is that most PPC campaigns fail but if you advertise correctly, it can also be extremely effective and profitable.

In PPC, every time your ad is clicked, sending a visitor or "lead" to your website, you have to pay the search engine (Google, Bing, Yahoo!, etc.) a small fee. When PPC is working correctly, the fee is usually a trivial amount but the visit is worth more than the trivial amount that you paid for it. In other words, if you paid $3 for a click, and the click resulted in a $300 sale, then you have made a nice profit.

Unless you company is a financial behemoth, you will most-likely never be able to sustain a long-term PPC strategy. The main reason

80/20 Rule		$500 Budget		$____ Budget	
	PPC	SEO	PPC	SEO	PPC	SEO

	PPC	SEO	PPC	SEO	PPC	SEO
Month 1	80%	20%	$400	$100	$_____	$_____
Month 2	70%	30%	$350	$150	$_____	$_____
Month 3	60%	40%	$300	$200	$_____	$_____
Month 4	50%	50%	$250	$250	$_____	$_____
Month 5	40%	60%	$200	$300	$_____	$_____
Month 6	30%	70%	$150	$350	$_____	$_____
Month 7	20%	80%	$100	$400	$_____	$_____

"80/20 Rule" as seen on p. 71.

is because you get charged every time someone clicks on your "Ad" or listed SERP page "paid ad" listing. If your goal is to steadily boost traffic and stay at the top, you'll be paying a lot just to stay visible on Google. In my opinion, your money would be better spent with a sound organic on-page/off-page SEO plan.

The one recommended way to try PPC is to utilize the "80/20 Rule" as seen on p. 71. I am stating it again as a reminder of how important it is to make a plan with a budget.

PPC in the long run could be very expensive but if planned correctly in conjunction with a solid SEO plan, it could work well. A lot of marketers like to use a rule in which I call the "80-20" rule. This is where you start a marketing campaign as follows. If you are solely marketing using only SEO and PPC, under this rule, the first month you spend 80% of your budget on PPC and 20% on organic SEO. The second month you would spend 70% on PPC and 30% on SEO. The third month you would spend 60% on PPC and 40% on SEO. You would do this monthly until the seventh month when you should be spending at 20% PPC and 80% SEO.

Using this "seesaw" plan, you get immediate ad awareness through PPC while taking a few months to build up a solid SEO game.

2) Another "con" is when your money runs out, you disappear from the top spot. This is in drastic contrast to organic SEO content

marketing that I recommend. Organic SEO is where you earn your SERP spot slowly, over time. Once you rank organically, and as long as your content remains fairly fresh and relevant, it will never disappear, and you won't pay a cent more than your up-front costs for producing and publishing. PPC on the other hand is "pay as you go". When you run out of money, you drop from the rankings.

How PPC works (in a nutshell)

When a searcher is looking for an electrician or electrical services, Google wants to provide, to the searcher, relevant, quality results. This is called the Quality Score and basically what it means is that Google, Bing and other search engines use a metric that influences ad rank and cost per click of ads. To determine the position of the ad on a search engine, each ad is allocated using a process which takes into account the bid and the Quality Score. As defined by Google, the "Quality Score is an estimate of the quality of your ads, keywords, and landing pages. Higher quality ads can lead to lower prices and better ad positions." This is one reason that it is so important to have a good website with individual pages for all of your products and services.

Another factor that pertains to the Quality Score is the keywords that you are using to setup a PPC campaign. If you use standard fare electrical keywords such as electrician, residential electrical, ceiling fan installation, receptacle installation, GFI, PLC's, etc., Google may see those keywords as not relevant, leading to PPC failure. 9 times out of 10, failure is because you list keywords without backing the keywords up with a page, on your website, that is compelling in nature and talks about the keyword. For example, if the customer is searching for "automation and controls", you should have a website page that specifically talks about "automation and controls". This gives Google the relevancy to make you an authority on "automation and controls" thereby placing your "Ad" first in line when a searcher is performing a query. If you are using

PPC along with general fare keywords <u>without</u> a website to back up your "talk", Google really doesn't care for this. In the long-term, this is a recipe for failure because Google wants to place the best suited "Ad" before the searcher or it even makes Google look bad in the long run.

The correct way to setup a PPC campaign is to be strategic with certain keywords and to set up specific ad groups for each one of your services that you offer. Follow these rules for better success next time you are running a PPC campaign.

• For example, you need to group all of the residential electrical related keywords together, and the industrial (automations, controls, PLC's, etc.) together.

Residential electrician, ground fault circuit interrupter, GFI, landscaping lighting, fan switches, ceiling fans, and more, need to be grouped together. Do not mix this with Industrial or Commercial.

• You need to write the Ad text specific to the sector of the electrical work that you are providing: residential, commercial, retail, industrial, etc.

• Once the searcher clicks on your Ad, it must take them to a website page that is relevant to the Ad. You must have fresh, relevant content that matches the query that the searcher is performing.

By doing all of this, your Quality Score is better in the eyes of the search engine (Google, Yahoo!, Bing, etc.,) therefore making you and your electrical company more relevant for the searcher.

By doing all of this, your Quality Score is better in the eyes of the search engine (Google, Yahoo!, Bing, etc.,) therefore making you and your electrical company more relevant for the searcher.

Paid Ad listings through Google Ads (formerly known as Google Adwords)

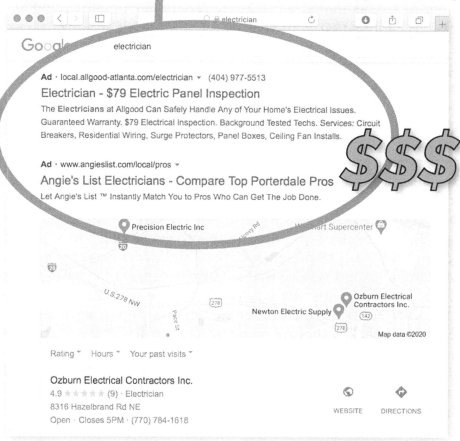

Benefits of PPC

The main benefit of PPC is the fact that you will most likely be seen at or near the top of a SERP listing. These are those page listings that you see with the word "Ad" beside it when you are searching for something. The following page shows a search for an "electrician". You can see the first page SERP results and there are two paid Google Ad listings. It is beneficial to show up on the first page of a SERP listing although it can be expensive. If the right person clicks your "well scripted and high Quality Score" Ad, you could end up with a long-term, good paying customer. Another benefit of PPC is that you can apply geographic targeting and appear in locations that you want to do more work. You can target specific areas even down to zip codes or communities. Google's map is laser focused on the local community and you can be strategic in getting customers within a few miles of your target area.

How much does PPC costs?

It depends. If you are the only electrician in town that offers electric vehicle charger upgrades or installations, you may come out fairly inexpensively if you write your Ad correctly and have a relevant website page to give you a higher Quality Score. When I say relatively inexpensive, you may be able to get a "click" from a lead at or around $10-$15 dollars a click. (I did say it was expensive). If you are offering a service that is more widespread and prevalent such as ceiling fan installation, you will have to fight it out with many other electricians and your cost may be significantly higher, $15 to $20 a click. There are many factors involved such as competition in a specific market, population of the town that you are running an Ad in, the average income of the people in the town, and much more. If you think electrical is expensive, try being an accident attorney in a city like Los Angeles, CA. A single click could cost an attorney several hundreds of dollars and that doesn't even guarantee a customer. That is just for the click on the Ad. Google also looks at the profession and determines the average profit that a company could make off a "lead". In the case of the accident attorney, there is potential for thousands of dollars, if not millions. Google reacts accordingly.

If you do plan on doing a PPC campaign yourself, read a little more about it on Google's website. If you feel comfortable enough to do it, set a daily budget so as not to deplete your budget too soon. You can also find marketing agencies that will setup PPC campaigns for you based on a percentage of the Ad spend amount. Usually that amount is in the 10% to 15% range of the Ad spend amount.

What is Pay-Per-Lead (PPL)?

PPL is very similar to PPC except you are enlisting the help from services such as Angie's List, HomeAdvisor, etc., Searchers will go to these sites looking for a vetted, qualified, service provider. The member will their contact information with the site and the site in turn will sell the lead to you, the service provider. You are paying for leads from this site, hence the name PPL. It is very similar to Adwords whereas when the searcher clicks on the Ad, it could cost upwards of $15 or more for that click. With PPL, the membership site collects the searcher's information and contacts two to three service providers to "sell" the contact's information. Usually it is around the same price as if it were a PPC Ad.

All in all, both services are like going to an old fashion auction. The electricians are in the audience as the customers are paraded one-by-one and you get the opportunity to bid on them. the high bidder basically wins.

Notes

_____

_____

_____

_____

_____

_____

_____

_____

_____

_____

_____

_____

Did you know that the median annual wage for electricians was $56,180 in May 2019. The average pay is $27.01 per hour. This information is based on U.S. Bureau of Labor Statistics.

Question 27

Are you using a CRM (Customer Relationship Management) software such as ServiceTitan, Housecall Pro, etc.,?

Some electrical business and other trades love CRM Software because of the strong marketing automation features. Fortunately for you, the business owner, there seems to be no end to the multitude of CRM software packages available to small businesses. Many CRM software providers, such as ServiceTitan and Housecall Pro, specialize in the trade industry. These companies, like many others, offer a cloud-based electrical contractor software package that enables electricians to offer digital invoicing, leverage business data reporting, monitor marketing ROI, and more.

Some features of a good CRM software to look for include:

Email marketing
Lead management
Lead scoring and qualification
Landing page creation
Web forms
Marketing analytics...and more!

CRM software such as these are usually targeted more toward the residential or light commercial arena.

Some benefits of using a CRM software are:

1) You can create a single storehouse for customer data.

2) You can provide greater visibility for your team with sales, marketing and customer service processes.

3) A CRM software can help optimize customer communications and integrate into existing email management sites.

4) It can shorten the sales cycles expediting the cash flow.

5) It can improve customer retention.

6) It can help you understand and address the needs of customers.

7) It can lead to higher customer satisfaction.

8) It can automate tasks leading to a better user experience.

9) It allows you and your team to operate more efficiency.

10) If can help free up employees to focus on customer interactions and service.

11) By utilizing all of the services, you can do even more to help your company grow while satisfying your customer base.

The great news about this type software is the fact that you can integrate it into your existing marketing strategy.

To find out more about various CRM cloud based software packagers, go to these following locations.

https://www.servicetitan.com
https://www.housecallpro.com
https://projul.com
https://www.hubspot.com
https://www.cosential.com
https://www.jobnimbus.com
https://www.procore.com
https://www.coconstruct.com
https://www.basisboard.com
http://www.jobprogress.com
https://buildertrend.com
https://www.plangrid.com
https://www.pipedrive.com
https://www.crmevangelist.com/home/construction-crm/

> **Tip:** Make sure to carefully review each CRM software package before signing on. Most offer a free trial period and you should take advantage of that. Some are aimed more toward residential or light commercial (ServiceTitan, HousecallPro, etc.,) while others are aimed more toward commercial, industrial or even heavy industrial (Procore, Plangrid, etc.,).

Question 28

Are you using Google Search Control (GSC)? (fomerly known as Google Webmaster Tools, and Google Webmaster Central)?

Much to the happiness of us marketers, Google has given us (and you) a simple tool to understand and the best part about it, it's **FREE!**

This tool, known as **GSC or Google Search Control** can look at your site and determine what issues might be affecting your traffic, and how you can improve the site for better rankings and results. This tool has been around for a while and used to be referred to as Google Webmaster Tools or Google Webmaster Central in even earlier days. If you've see different terms, don't worry because they are refer to the same marketing tool.

https://www.google.com/webmaster

The great thing about Google Search Console, or GSC, is that it's completely free. And it's made by Google itself, so the advice comes straight from the source.

Here's how you can use GSC to maximize your SEO results.

1) Sign into your Google account. If you don't have a Google account (you do if you have a gmail account), it is free to open a new Google account at https://accounts.google.com/signup .

Make sure you're using your business (not personal) account if it's a business website.

> "A good company offers excellent products and services. A great company also offers excellent products and services but also strives to make the world a better place."
>
> - Philip Kotler

198

2) Go to Google Webmaster Tools at
https://www.google.com/webmasters

3) Click "Add a property."

4) Choose "Website" from the drop-down menu and enter the URL of your site. Make sure you're using the exact URL that appears in the browser bar. To be sure, you may want to open your website in a new window and then copy* the url in the browser's bar. You can then paste** the copied url into the "website" space.

To copy and paste on a Windows Computer:
***Copy (Control • C), **Paste (Control • V)**

To copy and paste on a Apple/Mac Computer:
***Copy (Command • C), **Paste (Command • V)**

5) Click "Continue."

6) Pick a way to verify you own your website (HTML file upload, domain name provider, HTML tag, GA tracking code, Google Analytics, or Google Tag Manager container snippet).

Tip: If you already are setup with Google Analytics, this will probably be the quickest way to verify your account and website.

7) If your site supports both http:// and https://, you may want to add both as separate sites.

7) If your site supports both http:// and https://, you may want to add both as separate sites.

What can I use Google Search Console (GSC) for?

Google Search Console (GSC) helps you monitor, maintain, and troubleshoot your website's presence in Google Search (SERP) results. You don't have to sign up for Search Console to be included in Google Search results, but you do have to sign up to see how people or "searchers" are utilizing your website in the search results. Google Search Console helps you understand and improve how Google sees your site so you can make necessary changes either to your website or to the way you are marketing your website.

According to Google, here is what Google Search Console offers to your marketing strategy including excellent online marketing tools and reports for the following actions:

- **Confirm that Google can find, crawl and index your site.**
- **Fix indexing problems.**
- **Request re-indexing of new or updated content.**
- **View Google Search traffic data for your website.**
- **View how often your website appears in a Google Search.**
- **View which search queries show your website.**
- **View how often searchers click through for certain keyword queries, and more.**
- **Receive alerts when Google encounters indexing, spam, or other issues on your site.**
- **Show you which internal and external sites link to your website.**
- **Troubleshoot issues for accelerated mobile pages (AMP,) mobile usability, and other Search features.**

This tools is excellent for you, if you decide to do your own marketing, or for an agency that you hire to market for you. As a business owner, you should be aware of it, become familiar with the basics of optimizing your site for search engines, and know what features are available in Google Search. This will help you communicate better with whomever you hire to market your electrical services company.

There are excellent videos on YouTube that will explain how to use Google Search Console. Just go to YouTube and search "Google Search Console" and you will see many excellent tutorials that will walk you through using GSC.

Notes

_____

_____

_____

_____

_____

_____

_____

_____

_____

_____

_____

_____

_____

_____

_____

_____

_____

_____

_____

_____

_____

_____

Question 29

Do you have any idea how much money you are spending (ROI) on marketing your Business? Monthly?, Annually?

As a business owner, does it ever feel like marketing expenses will never end? Over the years and even prior to the internet, there has always been someone or some company that is always trying to pry your hands from your wallet, in some form or fashion. Years ago, you used a lot of print media, business cards, newsletters, phone book ads, and perhaps the old "stick a piece of "marketing" paper under the windshield wiper blade" to win customers over. Nowadays, it's the same expense (or perhaps more) to digitally win customers over.

Do you have any idea what your marketing budget is?

View	Zoom 125%		Insert	Table	Chart	Text	Shape	Media	Comment	Annual Marketing Budget Template	Collabo

+ Sheet1

Category		Q1						
	January	% Of Budget	February	% Of Budget	March	% Of Budget	Total Spent
Ads	$ 3,884.00		$ -		$ -		$ 3,884.00
Online	$ 572.00						$ 572.00
Print	$ 347.00						$ 347.00
Posters	$ 839.00						$ 839.00
Billboards	$ 836.00						$ 836.00
Radio	$ 356.00						$ 356.00
TV	$ 934.00						$ 934.00
PR	$ 2,670.00		$ -		$ -		$ 2,670.00
Events	$ 839.00						$ 839.00
Conferences	$ 836.00						$ 836.00
Press Outreach	$ 356.00						$ 356.00
Sponsorships / Partnerships	$ 294.00						$ 294.00
Webinars	$ 345.00						$ 345.00
Sponsorships	$ 345.00						$ 345.00
Social Media	$ 2,932.00		$ -		$ -		$ 2,932.00
Facebook	$ 983.00						$ 983.00
Twitter	$ 346.00						$ 346.00
Instagram	$ 643.00						$ 643.00
Pinterest	$ 345.00						$ 345.00
LinkedIn	$ 379.00						$ 379.00
Google+	$ 236.00						$ 236.00
Content Marketing	$ 2,314.00		$ -		$ -		$ 2,314.00
Sponsored Content	$ 125.00						$ 125.00
Landing Pages	$ 258.00						$ 258.00
Blog Posts	$ 374.00						$ 374.00
Email Marketing	$ 287.00						$ 287.00
White Papers / eBooks	$ 983.00						$ 983.00
Reports	$ 287.00						$ 287.00
Website	$ 1,010.00		$ -		$ -		$ 1,010.00
Development	$ 236.00						$ 236.00

Why do I even need a marketing budget?

Henry Ford once said, *"stopping advertising to save money is like stopping your watch to save time"*.

Unfortunately, when it comes to advertising or marketing your company, you have to spend money to make money.

If you are new (or old) to the marketing game and you are afraid to spend a considerable amount of money, you must think about:

1) How much of the marketing can I do myself ?

2) How much money at a minimal are you willing to spend?

3) How much money at a maximum are you willing to spend?

4) How can I incorporate the "80/20 Rule" from p. 71 into my marketing budget?

5) Can I delegate this work to an employee or team member?

6) Can I delegate this work to a family member?

7) Can I find and hire a high school student that is a rising star in marketing, web design, SEO, etc.,? (Believe it or not, they're out there!)

8) Can I hire off the internet? www.fiverr.com, www.upwork.com

These are all valid questions that need to be addressed really before you even build out your website. Also note that the more that you spend doesn't necessarily reflect a better ROI. It is how you spend. Spend wisely and track your results. If a strategy isn't working, switch to a different strategy. As marketing continues to evolve, strategies evolve also. A strategy that works today might not work tomorrow. Your marketing budget has to be setup to withstand ebs and flows of the marketing world.

How much should I budget for marketing?

The simple answer is around 5 percent.

Rules of Thumb for Marketing Investments

As a general rule of thumb, companies like yours should spend around 5 percent of their total, gross revenue on marketing just to maintain their current position. Companies looking to grow or gain greater market share should budget a higher percentage— usually around 10 percent or even as high as 15%. All this also depends on your products and services that you are trying to promote. If you are the only electrical services provider in your area for Siemens' controls, you may not have to spend as much on marketing and you can refer more on "word of mouth" or "repeat and referral". Just remember that the new "repeat and referral" is called social media and social media, although free for personal promotion, costs to advertise.

What should I expect to spend money for when marketing my electrical business? How much will this cost?

Here is a basic run down of today's marketing costs. Like I have stated earlier, most people, when referring to a website, think "if you build it (the website), they will come". It's just not that way. The website is the vehicle to promote your products and services. With any vehicle, you need fuel, maintenance, parts, labor, and more just to keep it running. It's the same with marketing

The cost of digital marketing in 2020

The following costs are industry averages for available marketing services. You will be able to find some categories priced "cheaper" or less expensive while others you will priced even higher. Hopefully after reading this book, you will have the ammunition to properly vet an ad or marketing agency or better yet, do most of it yourself. In some cases, you will be able to obtain reasonably priced services from sites like Fiverr.com or Upwork.com. In all cases you should read reviews and choose the most qualified individual at the most reasonable prices. READ REVIEWS!

If you ever feel overwhelmed by it all, remember that you can always contact us at help@PowerSurgeSEO.com and we will do I best to serve you! Everything that you are about to read about on the next few pages, we can provide for you at a reasonable price!

SEO
The cost of SEO services varies depending on what is included. Most SEO projects in 2020 cost between $750-$2,000/month based on the scope of the project. A one-time project will range

between $5,000-$30,000 and hourly rates for consultants fall between $80-$200/hour. Remember that in almost all cases, you get what you pay for.

PPC
Pay-per-click advertising (PPC)   5-20% of monthly ad spend

PPL
Pay-per-lead (PPL) - depends on the industry, category (residential, commercial, industrial) and the demand. Expect to pay $15 - $25 per lead from a lead agency. Because PPL agencies are typically like Angie's List, HomeAdvisor, etc., I only recommend PPL for *residential* electrical work. It only stands to reason that any commercial or industrial general contractor will most likely not use these services to find qualified electricians. Please note that even if you pay for the lead, you are only paying for the opportunity to bid on the job. For example, you can pay $20 for a chance to bid on a job against probably two other electrical contractors that have been invited by the PPL agency. There is always the chance that the other two contractors will offer a bid to the homeowner that is lower than yours.

In that case, you have basically lost $20, the initial price of the lead.

EMAIL MARKETING
Prices range from $50 - $5,000/month or $0.1 - $0.5/email
Some email marketing websites offer free services for 500 email addresses or less. As you increase your email list, the base price increases.

Here is a just a few email marketing service providers:

ConstantContact.com
Sendinblue.com
MailerLite.com
email250.com
HubSpot.com
ActiveCampaign.com
MailChimp.com

Tip: If at anytime you become overwhelmed, contact us at *help@PowerSurgeSEO.com* and we will help you out. Call us today at 1-888-235-4SEO (4736).

EMAIL VERIFICATION (email compliance - cleans up and validates email)
www.Neverbounce.com

SOCIAL MEDIA MARKETING
Prices range from $250 - $10,000/month+
(email *help@PowerSurgeSEO.com*)

GOOGLE ADS
Prices range from $50-$100/week
to $10,000/month+

WEBSITE DESIGN
$1,500 - $100k+ - (email *help@PowerSurgeSEO.com*)
Base website designs usually include 4-5 pages (home, blog, services, locations, contact). The more pages that you add, the more expensive the site will be. Ozburn Electrical Contractors, Inc's site at www.OzburnElectrical.com has over 100 pages that represent different products and/or services. Remember, for the sake of a strong on-page and off-page SEO strategy, that you truly need individual pages to represent your products and services.

WEBSITE HOSTING
Powersurgeseo.com - (email *help@PowerSurgeSEO.com*)
Globat.com - $4.44/Month - $100+/Month (See Site)
Hostgator.com - $2.75/Month - $100+/Month (See Site)
Godaddy.com - $5.99/Month - $100+/Month (See Site)

PRESS RELEASES
Prices range from $150 - $5k per press release
(email *help@PowerSurgeSEO.com*)

You can keep this expense down a little by writing your own content between 500 - 1,500 words. Use for special occasions, etc.

ANALYTICS
Google Analytics works great but an alternative is Clicky.
www.Analytics.Google.com, www.Clicky.com.

CITATIONS CLEANED UP (ONLINE DIRECTORIES)
Prices range from $250 - $1k per cleanup
(Fiverr.com, Upwork.com, Expressupdate.com, factual.com, Neustarlocaleze.biz, Google My Business, etc.,)
Also consider **www.BrightLocal.com** for DIY.
This has to do with your NAP (Name, Address, Phone Number). If your name, address, and phone number seems to be very inconsistent across the internet, you may need to do this. Try to make sure that you have at least 2 out of 3 correct and do not use P.O. Boxes.

WEBINARS
Prices range from $Free - 20/month+
You may or may not have to purchase additional equipment such as pc or laptop camera, earphones, microphone, etc.,

Here are a few webinar hosting sites worth looking into.
Zoom.com   Demio.com
WebinarNinja.com   Jetwebinar.com
GoToWebinar.com   WebEx.com
GetResponse.com   ClickMeeting.com
LiveStream.com   Google Meet (meet.google.com)

REVIEWS SOFTWARE AND SERVICES
SignPost.com BirdEye.com   Swellcx.com
Yext.com   Reputation.com   GetMoreReviews.com

PODCASTS
Prices range from $50 - $500 for basic startup equipment. Do a search for "Podcast Bundle" or "Podcast kit" on Amazon.

$Free - $50/month for Podcast Hosting site

Here are a few podcast hosting sites to look into.
  Buzzsprout.com
  Captivate.fm
  Transistor.fm

Tip: Use your SmartPhone to create quick videos for posting on Social Media. For added splash and video editing, contact our team at "help@PowerSurgeSEO.com"

Castos.com
Podbean.com
Simplecast.com
Resonate (https://app.resonaterecordings.com/signup/hosting)

TEXT MESSAGING (SMS)
Experttexting.com
Total Cost of Long Code SMS: US $0.0083/each text
Total Cost of Short Code SMS: US $0.012/each text
OneSignal.com - Push Notification Tool

PRINT MEDIA
Sinalite.com
Printingforless.com
PowerSurgeSEO.com

APPAREL
Queensboro.com
PowerSurgeSEO.com

MISCELLANEOUS
Fiverr.com
Upwork.com
PowerSurgeSEO.com

VIDEO EDITING
Apple (Mac) iMovie
Wondershare FilmoraPro,
Wondershare Filmora9
Fiverr.com

www.PowerSurgeSEO.com
help@PowerSurgeSEO.com
1-888-235-4SEO

PHOTO EDITING
Adobe Photoshop CC Lite
Affinity Photo
Get Free Images at www.Pixabay.com (must attribute author)
Fiverr.com

EDUCATIONAL
www.Udemy.com
www.YouTube.com

www.Lynda.com
www.SkillShare.com

Where do I start with a marketing budget?

It all starts with a pen to paper. The following two pages have a very simplified example of a marketing budget. I then included a page that you can carefully cut out and make enlarged copies on a copier. If you would like a print out of a similar marketing budget sheet, find one at www.PowerSurgeSEO.com.

Many of the forms seen in this book can be found at: www.PowerSurgeSEO.com.

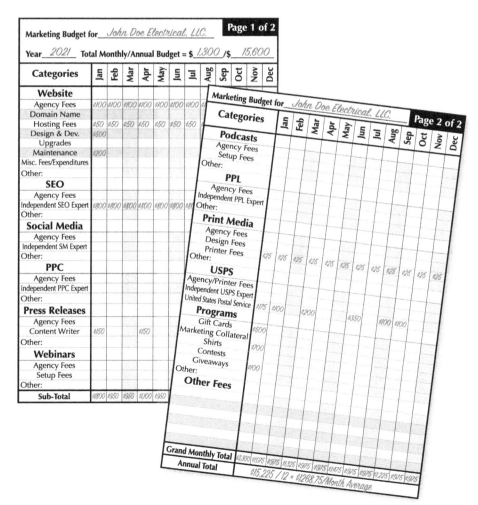

Marketing Budget for_____ **Page 1 of 2**

Year_____ Total Monthly/Annual Budget = $_____/$_____

Categories	Jan	Feb	Mar	Apr	May	Jun	Jul	Aug	Sep	Oct	Nov	Dec
Website												
Agency Fees												
Domain Name												
Hosting Fees												
Design & Dev.												
Upgrades												
Maintenance												
Misc. Fees/Expenditures												
Other:												
SEO												
Agency Fees												
Independent SEO Expert												
Other:												
Social Media												
Agency Fees												
Independent SM Expert												
Other:												
PPC												
Agency Fees												
Independent PPC Expert												
Other:												
Press Releases												
Agency Fees												
Content Writer												
Other:												
Webinars												
Agency Fees												
Setup Fees												
Other:												
Sub-Total												

Cut out and enlarge on copier and print on both sides.

Categories	Jan	Feb	Mar	Apr	May	Jun	Jul	Aug	Sep	Oct	Nov	Dec
Marketing Budget for_____ Page 2 of 2												
Podcasts												
Agency Fees												
Setup Fees												
Other:												
PPL												
Agency Fees												
Independent PPL Expert												
Other:												
Print Media												
Agency Fees												
Design Fees												
Printer Fees												
Other:												
USPS												
Agency/Printer Fees												
Independent USPS Expert												
United States Postal Service												
Programs												
Gift Cards												
Marketing Collateral												
Shirts												
Contests												
Giveaways												
Other:												
Other Fees												
Grand Monthly Total												
Annual Total												

Question 30

Do you feel overwhelmed just at the thought of doing your own marketing?

I've asked this before but I am going to ask you again. As an electrical services business owner, does it ever feel like marketing expenses will never end? Does it even feel like "marketing", generally speaking, will never end?

DIY Marketing is definitely not for the faint at heart and there is not only a lot to learn about marketing, it is constantly changing! At the beginning of this book we spoke about you, as an electrical contractor, receiving the electrical plans or schematics from a General Contractor. You systematically go through the plans and check things off as you go. Once you are finished, it's on to the next project. It's not that way with marketing. It is a continuous process of learning, switching strategies, testing strategies, paying for this, and paying for that, just to keep from falling behind.

You can succeed at DIY Marketing. I suggest that you start out with the first four steps of the "Marketing Pyramid" as seen on p. 60. You need to have a firm foundation in your website followed by a well-thought out SEO plan. This is actually enough to get you started. Once you get this under your belt, you can then try to expand on Social Media and maybe some PPC. If you go by the suggestions that I have made in this book, you can succeed without PPC. Even better, if you do decide to try both SEO and PPC, make sure to set up your Google Ads in a way that positions you for success. Make sure to study everything that Google has to offer from Google Ads to the Google Search Console.

I am willing to say that two of the most important things besides your website and SEO, is great keywords and striving to receive great online reviews. By reading this book, I hope that you can now comfortably answer the following few questions with no problems.

When it comes to marketing your electrical services company, what are you hoping to achieve and how?

_____
_____
_____
_____
_____
_____
_____
_____

Competitive Analysis
SWOT Analysis: (SWOT stands for Strengths, Weaknesses, Opportunities, and Threats)
Identify your strengths, weaknesses, opportunities and threats

_____
_____
_____
_____
_____
_____
_____

What is your Target Market
Explain who you will be marketing to: (residential, commercial/ retail, industrial, automation, etc.,)

_____
_____
_____
_____
_____
_____
_____

What are Your Company's Unique Selling Proposition

Explain what differentiates you from your competition: (e.g. PLC's, VFD's, Automation, Controls, New Residential, Old Residential Service, 24/7, Maintenance, Robotics, etc.,)

_____

_____

_____

_____

_____

_____

_____

Your Brand

Discuss how your brand is currently perceived (positive or negative, etc.,) and how you'd like it to be perceived.

_____

_____

_____

_____

_____

_____

_____

Marketing Channels

Explain how you will use the following channels to achieve your goals:

Content marketing: (Blogging, eBooks, Podcasts, Webinars, etc.,)

_____

_____

_____

_____

_____

_____

_____

_____

Social media marketing: (Facebook, Twitter, Instagram, Linkedin, etc.,)

_____
_____
_____
_____
_____

Reputation Management (Reviews): (BirdEye.com, Swellcx.com, Yext.com, Reputation.com, GetMoreReviews.com, SignPost.com, etc.)

_____
_____
_____
_____
_____

Email marketing: (ConstantContact.com, AWeber.com, GetResponse.com, MailChimp.com, ActiveCampaign.com, etc.)

_____
_____
_____
_____
_____

SEO (Search Engine Optimization): (Fiverr.com, Upwork.com, PowerSurgeSEO.com)

_____
_____
_____
_____

Explain how your SEO strategy will be incorporated into your marketing strategy:

_____
_____
_____
_____
_____
_____

Will you use PPC or PPL in your marketing strategy? If so, will you use the "80/20" Rule?:

_____
_____
_____
_____
_____
_____

Will you use "Google My Business"?

_____
_____
_____

You don't have to answer the following questions but I am listing them just to let you know that marketing can go very deep, as deep as you want to go.

In a Nutshell, Time Is Money and Expertise Matters. Need Help? Give us a call today at 1-888-235-4SEO.

Measurements and KPIs (Key Performance Indicators)

Detail how you'll be tracking the progression of your marketing plan: (Measurements & KPIs can be Google Analytics, channels, likes, bounce rates, shares, engagement, conversion goals, clicks, brand mentions, profile visits, etc.,)

_____
_____
_____
_____
_____
_____
_____
_____
_____
_____
_____

Marketing Strategy and Tactics:

_____
_____
_____
_____
_____
_____

Recap your strategy in a brief synopsis:

_____
_____
_____
_____
_____
_____

Who are you going to contact when you are looking for the right answers to your marketing problems? Help@PowerSurgeSEO.com or give us a call at 1-888-235-4SEO (4736).

Let's Recap!

You probably thought that this book would never end. If so, you are now somewhat familiar with the never ending saga of marketing your business. Unfortunately to stay ahead, you have to market your business daily. I hope you have been able to glean some helpful information from this book in how to market your electrical services business.

During the last 200+ pages, we have pointed out some very important features in marketing your electrical services company. Some, like levels 1-4 of the "Marketing Pyramid", are more important than others although all levels are important in their own right.

Here is a recap of some of the *key points of marketing your business.

*Please be mindful that everything in this book is "key" to your marketing success. It may be impossible to incorporate every suggestion in a "DIY" marketing strategy. If you ever feel overwhelmed, please seek the advice of a marketing professional. It's completely fine to do some of the marketing yourself while allowing others to help in other areas of marketing.

When it comes to your company being optimized for the Google Map Listing, this is critical. There are four (4) fundamental elements that you must initiate before getting ranked by Google.

1) Claim your Google Listing (GMB)
Your first step in optimizing your company is to claim and opti-

mize your Google My Business listing. Go to www.google.com/business to do this.

We discussed Google My Business starting on p. 122-129. If you need to, please refer back to those pages for a refresher.

2) Citations or Internet References

One of the most important thing that Google looks at when someone does a search query is the citations or references linked to your NAP (name, address, phone). In a sense, this is more important than claiming your GMB listing for the moment. It is critical to start working on the citations for your business. For example, let's say that Google's algorithm is responding (in microseconds) to a search query for an "electrical contractor near me". If your area has over 100 electricians, who is Google going to pick to be on the first page of SERP? Google's algorithm is looking for the business that has the most authority on the internet. This authority is built over time by a properly SEO'd website, videos, blogs, posts, citations and more. The "authority" signals point to the company that actually looks authentic based on all of the activity surrounding the company.

The way that Google can tell if a company is legitimate is to search across the citations and directories scattered across the web. For example, are you on Angie's List? What about CitySearch or HomeAdvisor? There are over 250 pay and free directory sites that Google sees as "authority" sites. You need to have your company listed on as many of these sites as possible.

If you need to a little more information about citations and directories, please refer back to p. 67.

3) Online Reviews (covered on pp. 130-132)

Reviews, especially good reviews, are one of the most important things that you can have to improve your Google SERP and, more importantly, your reputation.

Over 90% of consumers say that an online review is just as important as a personal recommendation from family or friends. Online reviews are extremely important because they have become a reference point for consumers across the US and the globe and because so many people trust them when making purchas-

90%⁺

of consumers say that an online review is just as important as a personal recommendation from family or friends.

ing decisions. Google's search algorithms are also falling in line with customer reviews. Google is now starting to put more emphasis on it's SERP based on your reviews and reputation. It's always a good idea after every job to ask your customer for a good online review. If they cannot leave you a good online review, ask them why and try to rectify the situation. In today's economy, you are only as good as your last bad review. One way to achieve a good review is after every job, have the customer fill out a "Customer Service Feedback Forms" as seen on p. 73. Also make sure to ask the customer if it would be ok to take their written review from the form, and add it to the website. If you have done your job well, most are happy to oblige.

"According to Google, 88% of Consumers Trust Online Reviews."

A very underrated way of getting more business is through reviews. From our internal testing, we have found that the companies that get the most authentic, honest-to-goodness reviews from their real customers tend to rank better in SERP. It is important that you put a strategy together that puts emphasis on getting good, solid reviews from your customer base. If you refer back to pp. 130-132, you can see more about how to create a strategy in getting good reviews on a consistent basis.

4) Respond To Reviews
Once you have a review from a customer, you need to respond in

a timely manner. It is important to respond to each and every review, both positive and negative, in a matter of hours rather than days. When addressing a positive review, thank the customer and invite them to always call you for any problem or service. Let them know that you are there to back them up.

When addressing a negative review, don't have a public dispute with them. It serves no purpose except to make you look like a bully or even worse, like you truly don't care for your customers. Simply let the reviewer know that you would like to talk to them to make the situation right. Tell them to reach out to you personally or better yet, you will be reaching out to them. Being proactive with how you respond can have a greater impact on future customers. Google even pays attention to customer review interactions between you and your customers.

5. Be Cautious of Keyword Placements.
When it comes to keywords, It is best to use your keywords 2 to 3 times per hundred words while placing them naturally and as seamless as possible. Placing too many keywords together is referred to as "keyword stuffing" and Google frowns upon this method of using keywords. Try to be as natural as possible when creating content that contains keywords.

6. Have a Strong Call-To-Action.
I would prefer that you have a "Contact Us Now" type of Call-To-Action button at the top of your homepage and preferably at the top of every page on your website. Also make sure to have your contact information legible just in case the lead wants to contact you other than from the website.

7. Make Sure Your Website Is Crawl-able and Indexable.
Crawl-ability describes the search engine's ability to access and crawl content on a page. If the search engine determines that the site has no crawl-ability issues, then web crawlers can access all its

content easily by following links between pages.

However, broken or dead links and dead ends might result in crawl-ability issues This would hinder the search engine's ability to access specific content on a site therefore resulting in lower SERP rankings.

Index-ability, on the other hand, refers to the search engine's ability to analyze and add a page to its index. Even though Google could crawl a site, it may not necessarily be able to index all its pages, typically due to index-ability issues. Both crawl-ability and index-ability play an important role in SEO.

8. Track and Target the Right Keywords.

SEO can be tough. It is not for the faint at heart and I commend anyone for doing it yourself. Fortunately I can rely on a team of experts to perform all of the SEO necessary to give my customers excellent results. One of the integral factors for ranking in a Google search results page or SERPs is knowing what keywords users (or potential customers) use when searching for content they need. In your case, the user could be searching for someone to install a ceiling fan or an electrician to work on a Allen Bradley control for an industrial assembly line. This is where conducting complete and comprehensive keyword research and mapping takes place.

Take into consideration your target audience. What exactly are they searching for? What keywords or "YouTube Tags" are they using when searching for that query? To research keywords, you can use the following tools: Google Keyword Planner, Keyword Tool, SEMrush, and Long Tail Pro. We use SEMrush for excellent results but there are other, less expensive tools as well.

An ideal short-tail or long-tail keyword is relevant to the main topic of your content and is used by your target audience when searching. This is a crucial step in knowing how users search and look for their answers to their queries. Like I said, SEO can be tough. I would advise you to seek a SEO marketing expert to help you when it comes to tracking and targeting the right keywords.

9. Write a Good Introduction.

When it comes to first impressions, good quality content works. Whenever you are writing content for your webpages, blogs, newsletters, press releases, etc., you need to nail the first paragraph. It is common marketing knowledge that If you lose the readers in your introductory or first few lines of type, you've lost them for good. Make sure to write a great, compelling introductory.

10. Add Social Sharing Buttons.

All WordPress sites have the capability for you to add social media sharing buttons. Please take advantage of this. It not only helps your website visitors to see your social pages, it provides invaluable external links to your site.

11. Improve your Page Loading Speed to 3 Seconds.

Page speed is a measurement of how fast the content on your page loads. This is extremely critical to retain viewers that are visiting your site. The "Golden" standard is around 3 seconds. Just try not to go over 6 seconds. Your site's speed is one of the factors that Google uses in it's algorithm to rate your site so the faster, the better. If you have done everything that you can to optimize the site's speed and it still is a little slow, you may have to upgrade your hosting plan to a Solid State Drive (SSD). You can evaluate your page speed with Google's PageSpeed Insights at https://developers.google.com/speed/pagespeed/insights/.

12. Mobile-First Indexing and Responsive Design.

Do you think a mobile responsive site is important? On March 26th, 2018, Google officially announced that they would be using mobile first indexing. This means that they now indexing websites based on their mobile version- not their desktop version (as was done in the past). It is extremely important that your website not only look good on a desktop version, but it is more important that it looks and performs good for mobile use.

13. Add A Strong Email Campaign.
You need to leveraged email marketing by collecting data from the customer that includes their email addresses. By pushing out a newsletter on a consistent basis, this will brand your image while providing content for your customers. You can also offer discounts or coupons for those who are on your email list. There are several email marketing companies to choose from and all do a great job of disseminating your information to your email addresses.

Here is a just a few email marketing service providers:
A) ConstantContact.com
B) MailChimp.com
C) Sendinblue.com
D) ActiveCampaign.com
E) MailerLite.com
F) HubSpot.com

14. Incorporate the 80/20 Rule. (see p. 71)
A lot of marketers, including myself, like the 80/20 rule. Once your website is up and running, you need to set your monthly marketing budget (e.g. $500). This amount can increase or decrease over the years. The 80/20 rule allows you to get up and running as quickly as possible but with a plan and within a budget.

Once you have determined your monthly marketing budget, for the first month, spend 80% of your budget on Pay-Per-Click (PPC) and 20% on Search Engine Optimization (SEO). Like the chart shows, the second month you will decrease the spending on PPC to 70% and increase the amount of spending for SEO to 30%. This pattern will continue until month seven when you are now spending 80% on SEO and only 20% on PPC. At this point, you can continue this spending as long as you want or as long as it is working. You can always adjust accordingly but this is one of the quickest ways to get you website noticed and perhaps get customers the quickest. You long term goal is to spend most of your budget on SEO as compared to PPC.

15. Pick the Top 10 Cities in Your Area

For the sake of great on-page and off-page SEO, make sure to select 10 target cities that you would like to expand your services to. Once you select at least 10 cities, build out 10 individual pages on your website that represent each city. While listing your services on these pages, also try to highlight some of the known facts of each city to differentiate one from another. Google will take this into account when a user is posting a query. **Here is an example of some cities that I used for Ozburn Electrical Contractors, Inc., located in Covington, Georgia.**

1) Covington, GA
2) Atlanta, GA
3) Conyers, GA
4) Athens, GA
5) Greensboro, GA
6) Loganville, GA
7) McDonough, GA
8) Commerce, GA
9) Gainesville, GA
10) Macon, GA

16. Try to Select Good Keywords

You may want to use the help of Google Keyword Planner (see below). Try to think like the customer as if you are going to perform a Google search for an electrician. Here is an example.

1) Electrician Brooklyn
2) Electrician near me Brooklyn
3) Electrical contractors Brooklyn
4) Brooklyn electrician
5) Brooklyn electrician near me
6) Electrical contractors New York
7) New York electrician
8) Electrician near me New York
9) New York electrical contractors
10) Brooklyn electrical 24 Hour

FIND THE KEYWORD PLANNER AT:

Make sure to use the Google Keyword Planner Tool found at https://ads.google.com/intl/en_in/home/tools/keyword-planner/

16. Hire Someone or an Agency To Perform Links, Citations, LinkWheels, Press Releases, Blog, PPC, PPL, create Content, create Videos and more!

We have practically gone over most (no where near everything) of what you need to know to get your electrical services business going in the right marketing direction. You can possibly try to do all of the marketing yourself, share the marketing responsibilties with others, or just hire an agency to do the work for you. If you do it yourself, you can save some big money but also it will possibly consume your time and possibly take time away from your family. If you hire an agency to do it all, the work will get done (hopefully) but it may be at a cost. If you split the work up, you can save money by doing the things that you feel comfortable doing while "farming" out the rest to individuals that specialize in certain aspects of marketing.

If you decide to "farm" work out, try these great options.

1) PowerSurgeSEO.com

My team at Power Surge SEO is ready and willing to help you and your business out by offering you the services that are mentioned in this book. You can always email us at help@PowerSurgeSEO or simply call us, toll-free, at 1-888-235-4SEO (4736).
We will be happy to help you!

2) Fiverr.com

If you didn't already know, Fiverr is an online marketplace for freelance services. Make sure to go to www.Fiverr.com and open up an account. Once your account is opened, you can do a search for a freelancer(s) for the following services.

A) Search Engine Optimization	F) Blogging
B) Citations and Directories	G) Blogging
C) Creating Content	H) PPC
D) Link Building	I) LinkWheels
E) YouTube Videos	J) and much more!

3) Upwork.com

Upwork, formerly eLance, is another website dedicated as an on-line marketplace for freelance services. You can join and basically perform the same "searches" as stated above.

4) Try not to hire from eBay. Unfortunately there are more
unscrupulous players on eBay who do not perform "whitehat" or above board services. Some hackers and unscrupulous individuals (even criminals) use their computer skills to harm or even damage computer systems. These people are called "black hat" hackers. "White hat" experts, on the other hand, use their computer skills to perform ethical computer services. Always choose "White hat" level individuals to do the work for you.

ATTENTION WARNING ATTENTION WARNING

Avoiding unethical digital marketing practices, individuals and agencies.

Unlike job sites that are usually clearly marked with warning tape, traffic cones, hard hat and safety vest restrictions, unethical marketing doesn't come with warning signs. Ethical marketing is honest and transparent. A good honest marketing firm or marke-teer does not use deception to trick someone into buying a product or service. It does not involve deceit to convince someone to buy something they don't need. **If you do decide to hire a marketing agency, here are a few questions that you need to ask yourself to be better prepared to speak to a marketing agency.**

1) What are my expectations for services and service costs: on an hourly rate, project rate or retainer? Have a realistic budget in mind.

2) How do you realistically expect to get to the "top" of Google? Strong SEO, PPC, PPL, etc.,?

3) Do you have any "successful" experience working with other electrical contractors? Do you have any experience working with electricians or contractors?

4) How will the marketer be paid? Paypal, Cash, Check, Moneyorder, Transferwise? (Be wary of Money-Orders). Paypal and Transferwise are reliable and proven. Cash is king but get receipts to show your accountant.

5) Will I have an Account Representative that I can speak to at anytime about my account?

6) What are your expectations of me, the client?

7) If you offer the same services to my local competitor, is there a conflict of interest? (Usually not if an ethical marketer)

Also, don't fall for "fake" unsolicited invoices of unknown marketing services. Fake invoices are running rampant among all trade industries where you will receive a bill for a marketing service that you don't recall asking for. Ozburn Electrical Contractors, Inc., recently got this fake bill from a fake agency. As you can see, there isn't a phone number and the address is only a P.O. Box. There isn't even a website address. They email address is not even specific to the company (yahoo). The unethical "marketer" is hoping that someone in accounting will open up

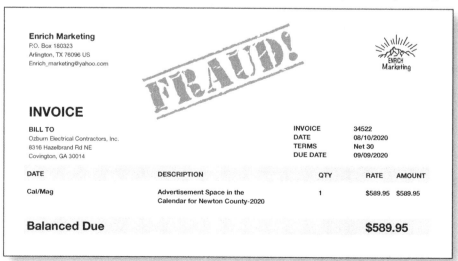

the letter and pay without asking questions. If the criminal just sent out 100 fake invoices a month and 10% paid, that would be almost $6k a month. Not bad for an evil day's work! I just want everyone to be wary that we live in a new day and time where, it seems, everyone is out to get your money.

Please guard all of your finances and have a redundant policy in the office whereas you check behind each other when you receive letters or emails asking for banking information, important data, etc., It is better to perform due diligence than to have to close down and reopen new bank accounts. Plus your local bank will love you for watching over your accounts.

Now you know the "marketing" road that is set before you. I hope that this book has given you enough knowledge to travel this road. I hope and pray that this is just the beginning of good things for you and your electrical services business.

Happy Marketing!, Ozzie

Connect with and/or follow me at:

LinkedIn - https://www.linkedin.com/in/ozzieozburn/

Twitter - @ozzieozburn

Instagram - https://www.instagram.com/ozzie_ozburn

Facebook (Personal) - https://www.facebook.com/GlennOzzieOzburn

Facebook (Power Surge SEO) - https://www.facebook.com/PowerSurgeSEO

Facebook (Get Viral! Marketing) - https://www.facebook.com/YourLocalMarketingAgency

Notes

Many of the forms seen in this book can be found at:
www.PowerSurgeSEO.com.

APPENDICES

Best SEO Keywords For Electricians

There is no getting around it, any SEO campaign you run for your electric company, no matter how brilliantly executed, stands or falls based on your target keywords. If you have selected the right keywords, you will get more and more organic website traffic from Google as time goes on. Choose the wrong keywords, and your competition will surpass you. But there is plenty to be excited about! Did you know that there are over 500,000 U.S. based online searches for electricians each month? By optimizing your website with the Top SEO keywords for electricians you are providing yourself with inbound leads that will only serve to complement the ones you generate through referrals and traditional advertising methods.

Here are the (high competition) keywords for the term "electricians" (as of August, 2020) in the United States - courtesy of the Google Keyword Planner. I am only listing 50 just to get you acclimated to what you will find when you perform a "keyword search" using the Google Keyword Planner tool.

1. electrician
2. electrician near me
3. electrical contractors
4. emergency electrician
5. electric company near me
6. journeyman electrician
7. local electricians
8. electrical contractors near me
9. electrical technician
10. electrical companies
11. industrial electrician
12. residential electrician
13. commercial electrician
14. electrical maintenance
15. master electrician

16. 24 hour electrician
17. licensed electrician
18. electricians in my area
19. cost to rewire a house
20. emergency electrician near me
21. find electrician near me
22. certified electrician
23. electricians forum
24. electric connection
25. becoming an electrician
26. quality electric
27. electrician services
28. budget electric
29. reliable electric
30. 24 hour electrician near me
31. electrician companies
32. custom electric
33. home electrical wiring
34. licensed electrician near me
35. local electrician near me
36. find an electrician
37. residential electricians near me
38. low voltage electrician
39. electrical near me
40. electrical construction
41. electrical panel wiring
42. electrical house wiring
43. commercial electrical contractors
44. powerhouse electric
45. best electricians near me
46. cheap electrician
47. professional electrician
48. qualified electrician
49. industrial electrical
50. construction electrician

> Make sure to utilize the Google Keyword Planner Tool. This tool will help you in determining best use of keywords.

When working with the above keywords, make sure to include your city in some of the keywords.

For example:
"your city" commercial electrician
"your city" 24 hour electrician
"your city" licensed electrician
"your city" electrical construction
"your city" industrial electrician
"your city" residential electrician
"your city" electrician
"your city" electric vehicle charger installation
"your city" automation and controls
"your city" variable frequency drives
"your city" custom UL cabinets
"your city" landscape lighting
and more!

> Here are a few other tools that you can use for keyword tracking. **Brightlocal, Moz, Raven Tools, SemRush, SerpStat, and Woorank!**

WordPress SEO (Free)
https://rankmath.com
Rank Math is a Search Engine Optimization plugin for WordPress that makes it easy for anyone to optimize their content with built-in suggestions based on widely-accepted best practices. Easily customize important SEO settings, control which pages are indexable, and how you want your website to appear in search with Structured data.

Here are few other great WordPress Plugins for managing SEO.
1) Yoast
2) SEO Pressor
3) SEO Optimized Images
4) SEO Internal Links
5) All in One SEO Pack
6) SEO Squirrly
7) SEO Post Content Links
8) Riderection

Many of the forms seen in this book can be found at:
www.PowerSurgeSEO.com.

Citations and Directories

Don't wait — add your local electrical contracting business to some of these business listings and directories as soon as you can. <u>Login credentials For Business Directory listings:</u>
(This creates backlinks (citations) to your site which is a good thing!)

Facebook.com
User Name:_____ Password:_____
****

Apple Maps (https://appleid.apple.com)
User Name:_____ Password:_____
****

Google My Business (https://www.google.com/business)
User Name:_____ Password:_____
****

LinkedIn Company Directory (linkedin.com)
User Name:_____ Password:_____
****

Bing.com
User Name:_____ Password:_____
****

Yelp.com
User Name:_____ Password:_____
****

Better Business Bureau (bbb.org)
User Name:_____ Password:_____
****

Foursquare.com
User Name:_____ Password:_____
****

MapQuest.com
User Name:_____ Password:_____
****

HubSpot.com
User Name:_____ Password:_____
****

YellowPages.com
User Name:_____ Password:_____
****

Angie's List (www.angieslist.com)
User Name:_____ Password:_____
****

Yahoo! Local (https://smallbusiness.yahoo.com/local)
User Name:_____ Password:_____
****

Manta.com
User Name:_____ Password:_____
****

MerchantCircle.com
User Name:_____ Password:_____
****

SuperPages.com
User Name:_____ Password:_____
****

YellowBook.com
User Name:_____ Password:_____
****

Thumbtack.com
User Name:_____ Password:_____
****

local.com
User Name:_____ Password:_____
****

kudzu.com
User Name:_____ Password:_____
****

HotFrog.com
User Name:_____ Password:_____
****

communitywalk.com
User Name:_____ Password:_____
****

brownbook.net
User Name:_____Password:_____
****

tupalo.com
User Name:_____Password:_____
****

LaCartes.com
User Name:_____Password:_____
****

2findlocal.com
User Name:_____Password:_____
****

ezlocal.com
User Name:_____Password:_____
****

ebusinesspages.com
User Name:_____Password:_____
****

Spoke.com
User Name:_____Password:_____
****

chamberofcommerce.com
User Name:_____Password:_____
****

CitySquares.com
User Name:_____Password:_____
****

Cylex USA (https://www.cylex.us.com)
User Name:_____Password:_____
****

yelloyello.com
User Name:_____Password:_____
****

BOTW (https://local.botw.org)
User Name:_____Password:_____
****

worldweb.com
User Name:_____ Password:_____
****

ibegin.com
User Name:_____ Password:_____
****

fyple.com
User Name:_____ Password:_____
****

company.com
User Name:_____ Password:_____
****

CallUpContact.com
User Name:_____ Password:_____
****

finduslocal.com
User Name:_____ Password:_____
****

MyHuckleberry.com
User Name:_____ Password:_____
****

hub.biz
User Name:_____ Password:_____
****

where2go.com
User Name:_____ Password:_____
****

CityInsider.com
User Name:_____ Password:_____
****

n49.com
User Name:_____ Password:_____
****

MySheriff.ca
User Name:_____ Password:_____
****

opendi.us
User Name:_____Password:_____

****

bizhwy.com
User Name:_____Password:_____

****

smartguy.com
User Name:_____Password:_____

****

wherezit.com
User Name:_____Password:_____

****

DiscoverOurTown.com
User Name:_____Password:_____

****

nexport.com
User Name:_____Password:_____

****

USdirectory.com
User Name:_____Password:_____

****

wowcity.com
User Name:_____Password:_____

****

Bizadee.com
User Name:_____Password:_____

****

wand.com
User Name:_____Password:_____

****

MapQuest.com
User Name:_____Password:_____

****

YellowPages.com
User Name:_____Password:_____

****

JustLanded.com
User Name:_____ Password:_____
****

CitySearch.com
User Name:_____ Password:_____
****

WhitePages.com
User Name:_____ Password:_____
****

SuperPages.com
User Name:_____ Password:_____
****

JustDial.com
User Name:_____ Password:_____
****

YellowBook.com
User Name:_____ Password:_____
****

InsiderPages.com
User Name:_____ Password:_____
****

YellowBot.com
User Name:_____ Password:_____
****

DexKnows.com
User Name:_____ Password:_____
****

StoreBoard.com
User Name:_____ Password:_____
****

Cortera.com
User Name:_____ Password:_____
****

Cylex.US.com
User Name:_____ Password:_____
****

SaleSpider.com
User Name:_____Password:_____
****

ShowMeLocal.com
User Name:_____Password:_____
****

Localeze.com
User Name:_____Password:_____
****

CitySquares.com
User Name:_____Password:_____
****

LocalStack.com
User Name:_____Password:_____
****

Yasabe.com
User Name:_____Password:_____
****

InfoUSA.com
User Name:_____Password:_____
****

infobel.com
User Name:_____Password:_____
****

botw.org
User Name:_____Password:_____
****

aboutus.com
User Name:_____Password:_____
****

www.spoke.com
User Name:_____Password:_____
****

blogarama.com
User Name:_____Password:_____
****

bingplaces.com
User Name:_____ Password:_____
****

smallbusiness.yahoo.com/local
User Name:_____ Password:_____
****

business.foursquare.com
User Name:_____ Password:_____
****

www.yellowpages.com
User Name:_____ Password:_____
****

www.chamberofcommerce.com
User Name:_____ Password:_____
****

www.hotfrog.com
User Name:_____ Password:_____
****

www.merchantcircle.com
User Name:_____ Password:_____
****

www.superpages.com
User Name:_____ Password:_____
****

nextdoor.com
User Name:_____ Password:_____
****

www.elocal.com
User Name:_____ Password:_____
****

www.dexknows.com
User Name:_____ Password:_____
****

www.alignable.com
User Name:_____ Password:_____
****

www.local.com
User Name:_____Password:_____
****

www.b2byellowpages.com
User Name:_____Password:_____
****

Site Name: _____
User Name:_____Password:_____
****

Site Name: _____
User Name:_____Password:_____
****

Site Name: _____
User Name:_____Password:_____
****

Site Name: _____
User Name:_____Password:_____
****

Site Name: _____
User Name:_____Password:_____
****

Site Name: _____
User Name:_____Password:_____
****

Site Name: _____
User Name:_____Password:_____
****

Site Name: _____
User Name:_____Password:_____
****

Site Name: _____
User Name:_____Password:_____
****

Site Name: _____
User Name: _____ Password: _____
****

Site Name: _____
User Name: _____ Password: _____
****

Site Name: _____
User Name: _____ Password: _____
****

Site Name: _____
User Name: _____ Password: _____
****

Site Name: _____
User Name: _____ Password: _____
****

Site Name: _____
User Name: _____ Password: _____
****

Site Name: _____
User Name: _____ Password: _____
****

Site Name: _____
User Name: _____ Password: _____
****

Site Name: _____
User Name: _____ Password: _____
****

Site Name: _____
User Name: _____ Password: _____
****

Site Name: _____
User Name: _____ Password: _____

Many of the forms seen in this book can be found at:
www.PowerSurgeSEO.com.

As I stated starting on p. 9 of this book, my goal was to basically give you a blueprint of how to lay out your own marketing plan. My intentions were to show you how to effectively market your electrical business (or any other business) either online or through print marketing. I am really excited that I was able to author a book to share information that a lot of marketers do now want to share or, if so, share for a price.

Although marketing is always changing, the information that you have studied is good, solid, reliable information that, if implemented correctly, will have an impact on the growth of your electrical services company. Although this information is not a secret, you would have to pry this amount of information from most marketers and it would literally take months to obtain all of this information from sources online. _It is just that valuable!_

I pray that the information that you glean from this book will make you not only a profitable business, but one that is able to give back to your community and your country. If at anytime you feel discouraged, just know that my team of experts at Power Surge SEO and Get Viral! Marketing or here to help you. Feel free to reach out to us at anytime for help. Have a great day and let's get to work!

Thanks,

Glenn Osborne

Feeling Overwhelmed with Marketing?

Schedule an Assessment & Marketing Strategy Call with
PowerSurge SEO Today! Call 1-888-235-4SEO (4736).

Schedule an Assessment and get the following...

- Free Website SEO Audit
- Custom Keyword List
- Website Optimization Cheat Sheet
- Website Conversion Review
- Free 30 Minute
  "One-On-One" Conversation

For more information on how we can help you turn around
your marketing, call 1-888-235-4SEO (4736) or send us an
email at help@PowerSurgeSEO.com.

We Specialize in Helping Electricians!

Call us today at
1-888-235-4SEO(4736)
www.PowerSurgeSEO.com

Feeling Overwhelmed with Life?

Speaking of being overwhelmed, I would be remiss if I did not do my due diligence and mention my personal relationship with Jesus Christ, my Savior. Back in 1986, while a Senior at the University of Georgia, I accepted Him as my Lord and Savior and life has never been the same. The world is basically the same but I now have a different outlook on this world and, more importantly, beyond this world. We live in a broken world full of troubled souls during troubling times. You can find solace in knowing what and where your future holds. If you do not have a personal relationship with the creator of man and universe, I welcome you to begin a relationship today.

I'll leave it here with this one verse that you have probably heard before. Hear it in a different way today...with your heart.

"For God so loved the world, that he gave his only begotten Son, that whosoever believeth in him should not perish, but have everlasting life." - John 3:16

He Specializes in Helping People!

If you would like to learn more about this Jesus, go to https://powersurgeseo.com/life/

National Suicide Prevention Lifeline
Available 24 hours.
English and Spanish
1-800-273-8255

CONTACT THE AUTHOR

 If you would like to contact Glenn "Ozzie" Ozburn for an opportunity to hear him speak at your event, contact him today at 1-888-235-4SEO (4736). Glenn is a great guy and he loves meeting new friends and in most cases, he would be honored to speak and share marketing and life tips.

Made in the USA
Monee, IL
10 January 2022

87642090R00138